Readings in Educational Management

JOHN M. GOODE, EDITOR

Readings in Educational Management

101278

amacom

A Division of American Management Associations

INTERNATIONAL STANDARD BOOK NUMBER: 0-8144-5323-6

LIBRARY OF CONGRESS CATALOG CARD NUMBER: 73–80183

First printing

Preface

DURING THE PAST several years educators have become acutely aware that there must be a better way to run schools. The profession has become uneasy about its inability to resolve its internal problems as well as to react to the public outcry about educational costs and to deal with the social issues inundating education. One frequent suggestion is that education should look to the management field to improve its capabilities in coping with its problems. As a former director of planning for a state department of education, I was concerned about the lack of materials designed specifically for educators. Thus the problem is not a *shortage* of material but a shortage of *appropriate* materials, available in the right place at the right time. The typical professional materials that cross the desk of the school administrator provide no guidance on management or the decision-making process, which is the major purpose of administration. The subjects of these materials are confined to the content of education and the broad range of sociological implications of education.

This book was written to help fill the need for materials appropriate to the administrative needs of the educator, and is written in the specialized language of the educator. As a participant, speaker, and designer of meetings to enhance the management capabilities of educational administrators, I quickly saw the need for learning materials that would serve as an entry point to the field of management. These meetings serve to whet the participants' appetite for printed materials appropriate for reference and self-development. Unfortunately, the classics in the field of management are not widely known in the education community. Those management materials that are available to the educator frequently are bogged down in management jargon that creates a semantic barrier.

Until now the needed resources were widely scattered throughout the professional literature. Over a period of several years the American Management Associations has collected a considerable quantity of management materials that are used for instructional purposes in its wide variety of programs. Those materials served as a starting point in the collection of readings for this book.

The practitioners of educational management constitute the second audience for which this book was written. Traditionally, trained educational administrators have learned that systems-oriented management books are not directly applicable to their needs, nor can they find a resource to meet their need for a general understanding of management. This book provides a bridge that will enable the educational administrator to enter the world of professional management. The collection shows the major features of the new intellectual territory called professional management and identifies the major pinnacles and valleys of the new geography. It is not meant to be a major treatise to explain the intricate details of professional management. In a volume of this size it is possible to provide only a general guide and to mark the dangerous curves. For the educational administrator to function comfortably in the world of educational management, he needs to examine in great detail the multifaceted concepts of professional management. This book will provide him with the means for acquiring entry-level skills.

The third major audience that will find the book useful comprises the students of educational management. The articles deal with the broad concepts of management as they apply to education, and will introduce the student to some of the leading authorities in the field. The readings will not, in and of themselves, enable the student to claim himself either a scholar of educational management or a practitioner of educational management, but they will provide a background to help him become a scholar and/or a practitioner.

Every effort has been made to insure that the articles reflect the current state of the art. When the selections were made each decision was unique; that is, no two individuals could select or organize the materials in an identical manner. The basic criteria for selection were ease of understanding and readability. The articles were gathered from a wide variety of sources, including professional education and management journals and books as well as government documents. With the exception of a few classics, the papers originally were published between 1969 and 1972. No claim is made that the search of the literature was exhaustive.

Many people deserve credit for their contributions to this book. I alone deserve credit for the errors, both of omission and of commission. The debt to others is especially great in a book that attempts to gather the thoughts and writings of others into a new format. Without their generous assistance the book would not have been possible. Other people have shared their ideas through countless hours of discussion and debate to help clarify for me the basic concepts of management. It is impossible to acknowledge this debt to everyone who helped shape the ideas expressed in the following pages, but to Franklyn Barry, Desmond Cook, Raymond Klawuhn, Michael Kipp, Alexander Basso, Carolyn Edwards, William Stinson, Marshall Brooks, Ann Taylor, Roger Schurrer, Duane Dillman, Annette Greene, and Guilbert Hentschke, I am especially indebted. They have challenged my thinking as employer, employees, teachers, students, confidants, and most of all as friends. This book would not have been possible without the assistance and encouragement of Mary Hill. Special thanks goes to my family, Carolyn, Kent, Brad, and Stacey, who have suffered the pains of literary birth.

John M. Goode

Contents

I

Introduction

"EDUCATION DOESN'T MAKE much difference any more!" "Everybody's trying to run the schools!" "I am just trying to hang on till I retire!" These cynical, bitter comments are all too common among America's educators. No one can doubt that the management of the educational enterprise is going to change and become even more complex. The forces causing these changes have roots that go far beyond the scope of this book. To grasp the magnitude of the problem, one has only to consider the proliferation of books condemning American education, the volume of media coverage, the taxpayer revolt, the use of the courts to arbitrate educational decisions, and the militancy of both teachers and pupils. These forces are not exclusive to the field of education, but they are like the straw that is bending the camel's back, if not breaking it. At best, the pressures exerted on the manager prove a most unwelcome addition. These pressures are presenting an ultimatum to the educator: Improve the management of schools or else! The "or else" can mean drastically curtailed programs, shorter school years, increased political interference, or any of the cataclysms that seem to lurk behind every management decision.

The mandate is clear: If education is to maintain its viability as a public institution, it must become more responsive to the needs of the public and the pressure of the community. The mandate can be restated by simply saying that education must be managed more professionally. These threats to the viability of education are not new to educators. However, the cry of the critics strikes an increasing number of sensitive responses by both the public and those in the profession.

These currents and countercurrents have been only partly responsible for the interest in management evidenced by educators. The very size of the organizations that have been developed to service the educational needs of young people is truly impressive. They are among the largest organizations ever created by man. The schools have the largest payrolls and involve more people than any other organization in most communities. They also operate the largest transportation systems, the largest restaurants, and in some cases the largest baby-sitting services in virtually any community. The size and complexity of these separate enterprises force administrators to search for new and better means of administrating their school systems. Most educators believe that professional management techniques will help them carry out their responsibilities more effectively. It is hard to underestimate the potential results of this desire for professional management by educators as they attempt to improve their educational systems. By using the management techniques that have been proved in other fields, educational leaders will more quickly and effectively develop solutions to today's most critical problems. Historically, educators have looked to improved management procedures to resolve their most pressing problems, which has resulted in equating management with crisis treatment rather than crisis prevention. Such a narrow definition of the role of management principles has limited management's application in the field of education.

Improved management techniques will enable administrators to improve the education of children. No other reason for modifying administrative techniques is so powerful or has the clarity of purpose that attracts support. Although the more visible stimuli for improving educational management have come from outside the education field, self-generated force has the greatest potential for substantive impact. It is this force that will enable educators to mount management improvement programs to alleviate the management problems of education.

Through good management practices, the probability of appropriate decisions will be increased but never to the point of certainty. Good management practices will never neutralize the effect of bad decisions. The educational administrator who is looking for the latest-model panacea for the ills of education will not find it in the use of improved management practices. The most probable outcome of improved management is greater opportunity to solve the significant problems of education by means of a rational approach that enables the administrator to focus on desired outcomes.

BENEFITS OF IMPROVED MANAGEMENT

Sound management procedures will not solve the problems of education, but they will provide specific results that will enable the administrator to increase his effectiveness. The most important benefit of good management for a school system is the ability to reach timely, valid decisions. If decisions are not available on a timely basis, serious consequences frequently result. The need for appropriately timed decisions grows as the complexity of the educational environment increases. A review of recent newspapers will provide an impressive list of articles documenting the problems that can develop from delayed decisions in the areas of finance, student unrest, and teacher militancy.

Another important benefit of good management practices is the development of a method of resource allocation based on anticipated outcomes. Often, resources have been allocated on the basis of need or by equal treatment of all clients. The allocation of resources on the basis of anticipated results makes it possible to maximize the benefits of limited resources. It is probably too much to ask of any administrative procedure to decrease the actual cost of education; however, increased efficiency and improved quality of education are predictable results of good management.

Good management procedures also enable the educator-manager to evaluate the effectiveness of the school system's programs. The key element necessary for evaluation is clearly stated objectives, which are an important part of a management system. The evaluation process provides the educational manager with a yardstick to provide information on which program and resource allocation decisions can be based. Without planning and the other management procedures, the essential information is not available.

An important product of good management is that it provides a mechanism for the manager to plan his reaction to programs and activities before they take place. With inferior management procedures, consequences become evident after the action has taken place, and the manager is frequently on the defensive. Using adequate management procedures, especially planning, the manager can avoid potential disaster as well as improve the general quality of his decisions with his capability to carefully examine the possible results of decisions. Thus he is able to be nondefensive and can decrease the possibility of both personal and professional criticism.

One of the more critical results of effective management is the clear, visible allocation of responsibility for the actions of the organization. During the past few years the cry for increased accountability in education has reached a crescendo. The clear-cut accountability demanded by the public is a natural product of the educational management system. Although this is an important product, management should be valued for its assistance in improving the education of children; it should not be regarded as a public relations tool.

THE IMPACT OF MANAGEMENT ON THE MANAGER

Improved management practices will not solve all the manager's problems, they will not make him healthy, wealthy or wise, nor will they enable him to achieve greater status in his organization. In fact, they may cause him discomfort and even pain. The professional manager is forced to look at the future of his organization; he cannot afford the luxury of burying his head in the sand to avoid the reality of the educational world. He is held accountable for the success or failure of his organization, and as the decision-making process is clearly defined his bad decisions are as visible as his good decisions.

From the point of view of the manager as a person, a compelling reason for establishing good management procedures in his organization is the opportunity for success they provide him. The careful delineation of objectives and strategies makes it easy to determine if the efforts of the manager have benefited the school system and the students. He is able to gain self-satisfaction from achievement that is not possible without good management. Public criticism of education in the past few years has made the need for the ego reinforcement of educational administrators more important to them than ever before. With an opportunity for success available to the manager, a powerful motivating force for achieving that success assures benefits for the students served by the school system. As organizations grow larger and more complex, the opportunity for individual achievement must be built into the management system if educators are to be happy and effective in their work.

WHAT IS EDUCATIONAL MANAGEMENT?

The basic concepts of educational management are as broad and as vague as the basic concepts in other specialized fields. The concepts of educational management differ from the concepts of general management only in terminology and in techniques of application. For the purposes of this book the term "educational management" will be used instead of "general management." Examples will be taken from the field of education rather than from other fields of specialization, with the exception of a few examples from business literature needed to illustrate a particular point.

Management has been defined in many different ways by various authors. A definition frequently used by the American Management Associations in publications and meetings is: "Management is the art of getting a job done through other people." This simplistic definition suffers from the inability to support sophisticated, logical program structures. It is, however, easily understood by the management neophyte and serves as a useful beginning for a discussion of educational management. The definition will be used throughout the book and is consistent with the theme of the articles that constitute this book.

Although the definition is simple in form, it is broad in its impact. It implies that the manager needs skills in the areas of human relations, public relations, organization, control, budgeting, fiscal management, and most of all planning. The definition implies the single most important characteristic of a manager: He is a person who makes things happen. The concept that a manager is a problem preventer rather than a problem solver is also included in the definition. A manager brings decisions into being and is not satisfied to let decisions be made by default. In summary, the effective manager makes the critical difference between organizational success or failure.

The principles of educational management can be categorized into three areas of activity: planning, organizing, and controlling. This categorization is useful when management is considered as a concept and when the principles of management are applied. With the categorization of management into these three areas, a more easily understood framework can be built on which to develop the concept of management.

Planning, the most important element of management, should occupy the majority of the time devoted to management activities. A simple definition of the concept of planning is determining where an organization is, where it wants to go, and how it wants to get there. Formalization of this process includes increasing the commitment of the people who make up the organization as well as developing the necessary decision-making capabilities of the organization.

The second major element of management is organizing. Simply defined, organizing is the division of the work of the organization. Imbedded in the concept is an understanding of relationships among people and how resources, decisions, authority, and responsibility are integrated into a division of labor. The subtle interpersonal relationships, job duties, performance standards, and available skills contribute to the manager's ability to maintain a viable, healthy organization.

The third major category of management is control. Everything the manager does, or causes to be done, to insure that objectives are achieved is defined as control. It is important that the neophyte manager remember that managers control *plans,* not *people.* Another way of conceptualizing control is: The plan is carried out through control mechanisms. Control activities are those activities that insure that the planning and organizing activities are not merely academic exercises.

ORGANIZATION OF THE BOOK

Many writers use the terms "educational manager" and "educational administrator" interchangeably. Throughout the book, "educational manager" will be emphasized; if the reader prefers, he can substitute "educational administrator" without significantly changing the content.

The principles of educational management can be used by the educator whenever he must get work done through other people. The principles are as applicable to department heads as they are to the superintendent of the most sophisticated school system. The management skills are the same, differing only in the magnitude of decisions to be made.

The book is organized around the basic concepts of management. The next chapter deals with the broad general concepts of management that form the overarching premises on which more specific management practices can be built. The three following chapters discuss the more specialized elements of management: planning, organization, and control. Concepts developed in these sections are narrower in scope and more specific than those developed under the general management chapter. The final chapter describes strategies for beginning the process of improving the management capabilities of an education system. It is important to develop mechanisms that enable the school system to continue its operation while improving the management capabilities of the school system without unduly interfering with the education process.

Each part of the book begins with a general discussion of its central topic to provide the reader with the necessary orientation to the articles that follow. Although the papers constitute a framework on which conceptual knowledge as well as pragmatic knowledge can be increased, they should not be construed as an exhaustive encyclopedia but as a sampling. They are not intended to magically transform the reader into a management expert; they are intended only to provide a basis for further growth and development.

John D. Kennedy's article, "Planning for Accountability via Management by Objectives," offers a concise description of management and its application to education. It provides excellent how-to-do-it instructions to improve the management of education. Although the terminology and format do not perfectly coincide with the organization of this book, the basic principles are compatible with the general concepts of management as we have defined it.

The second article is a composite of speeches from a program sponsored by the American Management Associations. It discusses content identical with the principles of management described in this book and provides a more detailed rationale for the basic concepts of management as perceived by the American Management Associations.

Planning for Accountability via Management by Objectives

JOHN D. KENNEDY

Director of Pupil Personnel Services
Duval County School Board
Jacksonville, Fla.

To anyone rationally viewing the state of the world in the year 1970 one fact appears to be as nearly constant as any: This is a time of rapid change in almost every dimension viewed. Every political, social, and economic institution in society is moving away from the institutional bedrock where it has been anchored for most of the nearly two hundred years the American republic has been in existence.

Given this state of rapid change in a time where change of any type, for whatever reason, is viewed as somewhat akin to the Deity, one of the most significant problems facing the managers of these institutions is that in some way they must establish a form of control on the rate and direction of change. Such control must exist for the utterly simple reason that the alternative of control is chaos, and no living system can remain in such a state. Homeostasis is one law of nature which refuses to be compromised for any significant length of time, and unstable systems either restrict themselves to the point where order is reestablished in their environment or they perish. When viewed in this light it is obvious that the only issues really open to debate concern control of change by whom, to what extent, and how. Questions about all three issues are to some degree philosophical and political in nature, but they beg for answers.

Reprinted from *Journal of Secondary Education,* December 1970.

The purpose of management is to make cooperative endeavors function properly and convert disorganized resources of people, things, and money into a useful enterprise. Ideally, managers conceive of the services or products an enterprise can render, mobilize the required means of production, coordinate activities both within the enterprise and with the outside world, and inspire people associated with the enterprise to work toward clearly stated objectives. This is true of managers in both private and public enterprises and continues to be true whether the enterprise's product is a service or marketable goods. While the final purpose of the public enterprise will differ from the profit goal of the private institution, managers in each sector can, and do, employ essentially the same processes to get their jobs done.

Modern management theorists define management as a combination of five functions:

1. *Planning.* Planning is the function that determines in advance what should be done. It consists of selecting the enterprise goals, setting objectives to reach goals, developing policies and procedures for designing programs to achieve goals, and devising logical, goal-directed program structures for budget evaluation purposes.

Logically, planning must occur before other sequences of the management function, but it cannot be said that the other remaining four functions must have been performed sequentially before the planning function begins again. Planning is a constant part of the total managerial process, with planning revisions being made as often as alternative courses of action are demanded during the execution of the other phases of management activity.

2. *Organizing.* The organizing function is the process whereby determination and enumeration are made of the necessary component activities required to achieve enterprise objectives. It means the grouping of these activities, the assigning of these activities to groups, departments, and so on. Part and parcel of assignment of responsibility for activities is the delegation of authority to individuals charged with that responsibility. Authority is the key to the managerial job, and the delegation of authority is the key to organization.

3. *Staffing.* By staffing is meant the responsibility of management to recruit personnel to fill the various positions in an organization. On the executive level, staffing involves the selection and training of future managers. Collateral to the staffing function is the requirement that management estab-lish a system of compensation, appraisal, and promotion.

4. *Directing.* In his function of directing, the manager serves primarily as a coach, guide, or teacher by supervising his subordinates in such a way that the objectives of the enterprise are met. This is done in a multiple number of ways, including the establishment of standard operating procedures, issuing directives, conferences—both personal and group—and performance reviews. Because an implicit objective of any enterprise should be development of the abilities of subordinates, the manager's directing role includes training others to do the directing function.

5. *Controlling.* Nothing demonstrates more clearly the need for careful planning than the function of control. It is not possible to determine if work

is proceeding properly if there is no expected progress against which it can be checked. A good plan will not only prescribe a measurement which makes sure the objectives of the plan are being met but will also specify corrective action in the event that there is failure to achieve objectives. In essence, the controlling function is a form of constant program evaluation and decision making concerning the need for recycling, or redirecting, of an effort, including slowing down or speeding up of action as circumstances demand it.

Much has been written and said about the proper sequence in which the five functions of management should be considered. It is generally conceded, however, that planning must come first because no manager can efficiently proceed without plans. Planning, by its very nature, is a description, a road map, of the way management should organize, direct, staff, and control. Even though there are no absolute sequences for functions, or line of demarcation when one function ends and another begins, it remains certain that the direction of action is dependent upon planning.

The primary thesis of this paper is that once the planning function has been completed, assuming it has been done well, all else is creatively secondary. What remains is a careful laying of operational blocks, which finally results in the manager's doing what he said he would do. An accurate description of the planning process involved in any particular management system is, in essence, a description of the system in its entirety. Therefore, the more closely a management system is able to relate tasks to desired ends, the more likely is planning to be meaningful. One system for accomplishing this planning intent of management is that of "management by objectives."

Peter Drucker is credited with coining the term in 1954, but if Drucker can be called the father of management by objectives, then George S. Odiorne can be thought of as the nursemaid who has formed and shaped the concept into maturity. In 1965, Odiorne published *Management by Objectives,* a book that many in the field of management science consider to be a significant milestone in the development of management systems.

Odiorne began his book by posing a question that others had asked: "Is management by objectives really a system?" He then answered this by saying: "Purists in systems design will probably ask: Where are the networks? Where are the 'three time estimates' of PERT? Where does probability analysis come in?" The answer is that there is nothing in management by objectives that excludes such subsystems if the circumstances call for their use. A general system of management, however—if it is actually to be used by the majority of working managers to improve results—should not employ special subsystems merely for the sake of being "systematic" in the esoteric sense of the word. In short:

1. It shouldn't overcomplicate and oversophisticate the function of being a manager, but should try to simplify as much as possible a job that has become extremely laden with data, methods, and procedures.

2. It shouldn't be dominated by its mechanics, or by recipes to be followed slavishly.

3. It shouldn't be so philosophical and speculative that its effects are beyond

measurement. Measurement of results is imperative because, ultimately, the purpose of the organization itself imposes a crude but effective measure. This measure is called profit in a business enterprise, and cost/benefit in a public operation.

4. It should be possible for line managers to use it without having to lean on staff specialists every step of the way.

5. It should be reasonably self-regulating and self-operating rather than requiring heavy inputs of fear, control, or direction from a few on top upon the large number below.

Drucker, Odiorne, and many others see the overall principles of management by objectives to be:

1. Rapidly changing social, economic, and political conditions create a need for systematic and orderly management of all systems so that each interfaces with all to the greatest possible degree. This applies not only to systems external to individual enterprise but also to those subsystems which constitute any macrosystem.

2. The most effective way to do this is to begin with a goal identification procedure on all system and subsystem levels, with all subgoals relating upward.

3. After goals have been identified, a procedure is established whereby each management level is assigned responsibility commensurate with that level's relationship to the overall goals of the macrosystem. System organization would be a function of the most efficient way to achieve both intermediate and overall goals.

4. Management behavior that accomplishes results (i.e., meets objectives that are goal-oriented) becomes the standard of measurement. Any management practice and skills directed toward these ends are allowed at any level of action because common methods of management may not work in different situations.

As Odiorne points out, "Management by objectives is not a technique that sounds reasonable in theory, but unfortunately hasn't been tried yet." Literally thousands of organizations, public and private, now employ this practice, and the trend is toward even greater application in the future.

Briefly stated, planning for management by objectives is a process that employs the following basic steps:

1. *Goal setting.* For the purposes of this article a goal is defined as a broad, long-range aim of an enterprise. Objectives, on the other hand, are more narrowly conceived, have a shorter, program-oriented time span of existence, and are quantifiable in measurable terms.

In the private sector, the owner, or directors on top management levels, sets very broad, encompassing goals. As division of labor breaks down functions of an operational program, subgoals are set by subordinate managers, so that each division and level develops goals commensurate with its responsibility for whatever part it plays in the total effort of the organization. In the public sector this process differs only in the fact that initially all goals are set by the political process, even in those public agencies that furnish goods instead of services. For example, a municipal corporation that produces electricity owes its existence to the political machinery that gave it birth, along with instructions to produce electricity. It may have the appearance of a private corporation, in that a board of directors manages it and decides policy for its operation, but unlike a private corporation, it has a charter that may be revoked by the same method it was created—through political action. Thus, if the goals set by the managing body are at odds with the political scenario at the time, these conflicting goals are removed by the legislative process, either by disbanding the corporation or by appointing new managers who will establish new goals more in keeping with the current political atmosphere.

2. *Determining needs.* Need determination is the first step in getting from broad goals to specific activities. It is the process of deciding where to concentrate action and is accomplished by reviewing existing programs in the light of new goals.

This is done by making some assessment of the current status of all existing programs and deciding how much is being done to meet a given goal even before beginning a conscious, concerted, comprehensive effort toward that goal. Once an assessment has been completed and decisions made as to how much is currently being done, the difference between the present state of affairs and whatever must be done to meet a stated goal is what can be properly called "a need." To define a need in any other manner is to state a goal. For example, to say that children "need" to read is either a goal statement or a reflection that a goal already exists and children aren't presently meeting it. Quite often a need is expressed in the form of a problem statement, but even this implies goal direction, for a problem is nothing more than a frustrating block to goal-directed activity. The difference lies in the fact that a problem statement usually implies an avoidance approach, whereas a need statement is couched in a more positive tenor.

3. *Setting objectives.* But what of needs? We may know what we need, but how do we define how we will get there? The questions we must ask are: "What will be done, in what time frame, and with what expected results?" When these questions have been answered on the simplest operational level, an objective has been formed.

By way of illustration, the Congress of the United States might declare a goal of the United States Government to be: "All citizens shall have comprehensive medical care from the cradle to the grave." Such a goal is certainly long-range, for theoretically it would continue for as long as American society exists. It is broad in that it does not delimit any aspect of health from the spectrum it embraces. However, it does not bring us one step closer to the reality it proposes because of the very nature of its scope. There is nothing to "zero" in on, no "meat" into which we can sink our teeth, no specific platform for an operational program that has defined limits. However, if we say that an objective of the public health program of the United States is to inoculate all children when they are born, with polio vaccine of the Salk type, we have described what and to whom we will do something. If we add that in the initial year of such a program the total inoculated will include 25 percent of all live births, increasing to 75 percent within a two-year period and 100 percent within a three-year period, we have quantified the objective by describing a measurement that tells when the objective will be reached and by what schedule. Finally, if we add that a certification of inoculation will be filed with all certificates of live birth, we have described an evaluation element that will allow us to know if in fact we did reach our objective.

4. *Developing a program structure.* It is obvious that hundreds, even thousands, of such objectives could be a part of the greater goal of comprehensive health care and that many will relate closely to each other. For these objectives to be converted into action, it is necessary that they first be grouped as homogeneously as possible into some optimum number of groupings and these groupings designated as program areas. As an example, the above objective concerning inoculation of children might be grouped with other objectives concerning communicable diseases, and this combination might be known as the "Communicable Disease Eradication Program." This program then becomes a part of an overall organizational pattern known as a program structure. Such an organizational configuration lends itself to traditional line and staff functions but has the added advantage of eliminating, to a major degree, the duplication of administrative and operational tasks connected with organization by fund source alone.

5. *Policies.* Before objectives can be translated into detailed plans for programs, policies must be established to define the scope and limits of operations. Policies are broad guides for thinking, but differ from goals in that they have the characteristics of marked boundaries. The policies of an enterprise usually describe such things as program priorities, target groups, and kinds of personnel to be assigned to a program. Other policies may describe the organization desired and the relationships of different programs within a total program structure. In effect, policies are a guide to thinking within a broad field where the area is determined by the goals and objectives already established.

6. *Procedures.* Procedures, like policies, are part of management, but procedures are more specific than policy. The prime purpose of procedures is to give a guide to action, not a guide to thinking. They seek to avoid the chaos of random activity by directing, coordinating, and articulating the operations of the enterprise. They help impose consistency across an organization and through time, and they seek economy by enabling management to avoid the cost of erratically functioning personnel slowing down the pace of operations. In addition, procedures define how authority is to be delegated so that subordinates can make decisions within the framework of policy.

An example of procedure, as contrasted with policy, may be seen by considering the following. An organization has a policy that states that all plans must be reviewed by a central planning council before submission to management for final approval. The procedures for submission and review would be spelled out in detail, step by step, so that the decision process would not be an ad hoc activity with resultant faulty review.

7. *Development of program plans.* A program plan lays out in detail the specific steps for accomplishing a mission and sets an approximate time for each step. Any program is composed of sets of subplans, and each subplan should have objectives relating to the overall objectives of the total program. These subobjectives are of a detailed nature and usually deal with procedures and methods concerning budgets, personnel, facilities, people to be served or product to be produced. The basic stages of program development are:

1. Divide into steps the activities necessary to achieve the objectives of the program.
2. Note the relationships between each of the steps, especially any necessary sequences of the program.
3. Decide who is responsible for doing each step in the program.
4. Determine the resources that will be needed for each step in the program.
5. Estimate the time required for each step in the program.
6. Develop a quality control system that will constantly evaluate the progress the program is making toward meeting objectives.
7. Develop a detailed budget based on the planned program.

LIMITATIONS OF MANAGEMENT BY OBJECTIVES

The enterprise manager must always be aware that in spite of all the thoroughness with which he establishes his goals and goes about planning, management by objectives is essentially a process that looks into the future, and there is a margin of error in all forecasts of the future. In this respect, the further in the future plans extend, the less reliable they become. However, as long as he recognizes these margins he will provide for alternative plans to enable him to switch within limits if need be.

Most limitations can be classed into two main categories: (1) internal and (2) external. Examples of internal limitations are:

1. Resistance of change in established organizational patterns by those affected by the change.
2. Limitations stemming from a philosophical difference between old established goals and new, different ones.
3. Resistance to change because of demands placed on personnel to learn new skills.
4. Unwillingness by informal power groups to surrender decision-making authority to new groups.
5. Unwillingness of management to write off sunk capital investment in existing equipment, labor, or buildings.

External limitations are:

1. Changing political climate on a regional, national, and international basis.
2. Changing technology.
3. Changes in the economy that reduce or increase available revenue beyond the limits predicted.

CONCLUSION

Deciding who should do what is one of the intriguing parts of the managerial function. In management by objectives it is an absolute necessity that these decisions be made in a systematic, clearly defined, measurable manner. This requires that goals and objectives be formulated and adhered to as long as the enterprise's efforts are producing products or services in such a way that those goals and objectives are being met.

The Principles of Management

INSTITUTE MANAGEMENT TEAM

American Management Associations

MANAGEMENT DEFINED

It seems desirable that men in management should be able to define specifically and explain clearly just what the activity is in which they are engaged. A doctor rather quickly can define and explain medicine. A teacher will waste no words in defining education. A labor leader knows and can tell you immediately what the labor movement is. Being able to define what occupies a good part of our lives gives tone, purpose, and challenge to gainful employment.

Management is the responsibility for accomplishing results through the efforts of other people. Further investigation discloses that there are many synonyms for the word, such as "administration," "supervision," "foremanship," and "leadership." They all have the same meaning, varying only in degree of responsibility. "Management" refers to any individual having responsibility for the activities of others, whether he be the chief executive of an organization with 10,000 people, or a straw boss with only three or four people under his direction.

At times, there is much confusion in the use of the terms "administration" and "management." There are those who speak of staff activities as being administrative and of line activities as being managerial in nature. Still others reverse that application. It seems essential that we clarify our thinking as to these particular terms.

Reprinted from *Management of the Education Enterprise* (Report of the 1971 Institute for Chief State School Officers), Stanford University.

In this presentation, the terms "management," "administration," "supervision," "foremanship," and "leadership" are used interchangeably. Wherever they appear, we refer to the same activity; i.e., responsibility for the accomplishment of certain results from activities assigned to the individual, through the efforts of other people.

The definition just offered is a brief one. Some have made it even briefer by saying it as follows: *Management is getting things done through people.* There is a longer definition. It was developed by a group of business executives and teachers of business administration who met for an entire weekend at the Schenley Hotel in Pittsburgh back in 1941 for the purpose of arriving at a common definition. With some slight change that has taken place with usage, the definition is as follows: *Management is guiding human and physical resources into dynamic organization units which attain their objectives to the satisfaction of those served and with a high degree of morale and sense of attainment on the part of those rendering the service.*

These definitions are offered purely for the purpose of illustration. Many other definitions from accepted authorities in the field of management are available. The principle stated here is that those in management should be able to define it. They should become acquainted with the best definitions that are available and, from these, form their own. There are many features of all definitions that are common. The definitions offered here are not offered as the most acceptable ones. They just happen to be those that we personally like and present as thought-provoking.

Management makes things happen. Management does not wait for the future; it makes the future. Managers are not custodians; they are architects. Nicholas Murray Butler once said: "There are three kinds of people in this world: Those who make things happen; those who watch things happen; and those who do not know what's happening." Managers are supposed to be in the first group.

If a manager wishes to know how effective he is, let him list those things that have happened in the last 12 months because he made them happen. Is the line of products and services any different? Are the costs any lower? Are the sales any higher? Is the profit any greater? Are the people any finer? Is the morale any better? Is the place any cleaner because of anything he did about it? Is he conscious of having any impact upon his environment and what takes place within it?

Frederick R. Kappel, former president and chairman of the board of American Telephone and Telegraph Company, spoke at Westminster College in Fulton, Missouri, in 1962. Mr. Kappel said this: "To have a part in significant enterprise, to be one of its movers and managers—in industry or in government—is not to fill some niche each morning and leave it each night as you found it. It is to help build and shape, to plan and to execute, to measure alternatives against the horizon and act on the course that judgment and resolution comment."

On the front page of the August 1968 issue of *The American Appraisal* "Clients' Service Bulletin," we read: "It is a part of human nature to hope for something lucky to happen, some facet of fortune that will give one an unforeseen advantage, a boost ahead. Sometimes such a chance occurs, but it is well to remember that success never comes to a man of its own volition. The ease or rapidity of success seldom just happens in this world—it must be brought about. The man who wishes to attain leadership must everlastingly develop and sustain an insatiable desire to satisfy his disciplined curiosity about his world and a painstakingly active determination to put across whatever plan of life he envisions."

Leaders think, act, and motivate. Followers do, object to, resist, or revolt against what their leaders want.

TWO BASIC ELEMENTS OF MANAGEMENT REQUIRED
TO MAKE THINGS HAPPEN

Management divides itself into at least two basic elements: planning and *controlling.* (See Figure 1.) While there are many other possible divisions, this breakdown seems to be the simplest and also seems to include most of the others. Such a division leads to a one-sentence statement of the *executive function:* A person who has supervision over other people is expected to determine what people are doing, select the most qualified people to do it, check periodically how well they are doing it, see that methods are found by which they can do it better, and discipline those who *will* not.

The manager or supervisor must *plan* his approach to the problems presented by the activities he supervises. He then must establish *media of control* that will assure him that the people under his direction perform to the best of their ability, according to the plan. Since human beings are what they are, performance will always lag behind planned objectives. This is why we have supervision. If mere planning would produce human performance in accordance with the plan, supervision would not be required.

There is one truth that has been learned by thousands of executives and supervisors that has a decided effect upon their administrative attitudes and practices. Its acceptance or rejection divides administrators into two distinct groups. If accepted soon enough in an administrator's experience, it saves considerable grief. The principle is this: *Management is not the direction of things, it is the development of people.*

Management is taking people as they are, with what knowledge, training, experience, and background they have accumulated, and developing those people by increasing their knowledge, improving their skills, and correcting

Figure 1

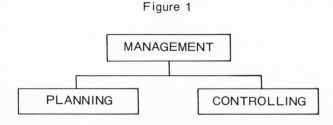

their habits and attitudes. Upon this improvement depends the success of any managerial or supervisory effort. In terms of such improvement, executive ability can be measured.

Put this principle to the test. *Try to think of any activity with which you are dealing that does not involve the development of people*—idle buildings; cold, uninteresting budgets; action to be approved, such as appropriations, requisitions, capital expenditures; analysis of statistics—all require the selection, the training, and the supervision of people in order that these activities may be handled properly.

The real objective of any management is to decrease the difference between actual performance and approved policy. The successful administrator establishes definite and complete policies. He has means of keeping advised of the practices of his organization as compared with the policies. If this is not true, his decisions as to the action to be taken in specific instances cannot be sound except by pure chance.

Every policy that is written, every plan that is developed, every decision that is made, and every activity that is initiated must be considered in terms of the capacity of people and the ability of supervisors!

It has been said that the executive function is to establish objectives, to determine how far present performance varies from objectives, and to discover means for closing the gap between actual performance and what is desired. In reality, that means that the basic function of a manager is to determine what people should, can, and will do; to analyze the actions of people so as to know what they are doing; and to develop and promote plans that will prepare and inspire people to do better than they are now doing. If this is true, it reemphasizes the necessity for human understanding on the part of the administrator. *Organizations must be constructed not as machines, but as living elements of human activity.* Administrative organization should provide situations in which people can work with minimum friction, misunderstanding, jealousies, and politics. Any organization should be so set up and directed that each person within it feels that it is an outlet for the productive and creative possibilities that lie within him.

The easiest way to get somebody to be what you want him to be is to treat him as though he were. If you want a baby to talk baby talk, then talk baby talk to him, but if you want him to talk English, then talk to him as you talk to others who speak English. If you wish a worker to have a broader interest in the activities of the organization, then discuss those activities with him as though he had that interest.

The huge administrative machines of the world are human machines. If you want to see the machines fall apart, take the human element out of them. If you want to see them accomplish the highest possible objectives, then develop the human beings that are in them.

PLANNING, POLICY FORMULATION

Planning includes policy formulation. (See Figure 2.) "Policy" is one of the most misused terms in organization circles today. It is often used to express

Figure 2

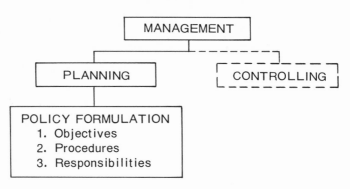

expediency rather than fact. There are constant arguments as to how definite a policy should be, as to whether it should be in writing, and as to whether knowledge of it should be widespread or closely held.

Words sometimes have their meanings changed with use and thus become confusing. It would seem advisable from time to time to check with the source of proper interpretation in order to keep words and terms from straying too far from their original intent. In consulting the dictionary (still a pretty good source of interpretation), we discover that *policy is a plan of action.* If properly developed, a policy will tell us what to do in a given situation in order to secure the desired result. It covers principles, aims, and conditions to be observed. It would seem reasonable to assume that if a policy is part of a plan, then to be of value, *it should be in writing.*

If policies are to be considered as mysterious, sacred matters, confined to the privacy of executive chambers, how can people down in the organization accomplish the results that such policies anticipate? *Naturally, there are many reasons and facts behind policies that cannot be made open information.* However, most organizations are willing to accept the necessity for secrecy on some phases of policy if other phases have been made an open book.

Plans must be drawn, or policies made, within the limits of which a company can operate. Employees down the line must advise management of the factors required to make that possible.

What Planning Should Include

If it is agreed that a plan should be in writing in order to be of practical value from a managerial angle, then it is important to consider what it should include. Little disagreement has been expressed with the principle that *a plan should include at least three basic parts:* (1) objectives, (2) procedures required to reach the objectives, (3) assignment of the steps of the procedures to individuals or organization units as definite responsibilities.

An individual may have in his mind the plans for a house he would like to build. He knows exactly what that house and its interior arrangement will look like. He knows every brick and piece of mortar, every closet, nook, and cranny. He studied magazines, and he has dreamed about it until it is vivid and clear in his mind. In his entire lifetime, he cannot build the house until he has had put on paper (1) an architect's drawing of the completed house, (2) a blueprint indicating how the house can be built to look like the drawing, and (3) what the carpenter is to do, the electrician, the mason, the plumber, the roofer, etc.

What is the difference between building a house and building an organization? It would seem reasonable to conclude that if it is true in the case of the house, it is equally true that a manager or supervisor will never obtain the results he is trying to obtain through the efforts of other people unless he has a plan, a policy, that indicates in writing the objectives to be accomplished (the architect's drawing), a basic procedure that will accomplish those objectives (the blueprint), and unless he has definitely assigned the steps of the procedure to individuals or departments in the organization as definite responsibilities (the electrician, the mason, etc.).

Objectives. A plan should include objectives that state the conditions that will exist if policy is properly applied. A marketing policy should disclose the amount and the distribution of desired business and the projected cost of doing that business, should provide for a just realization on that business, and should cover any other conditions that need consideration. An operating policy should disclose the type of service to be rendered to the marketing department and the consumer, a just cost at which such services should be rendered. A labor policy should disclose the mental attitudes, the type and amount of skill, the working conditions and relationships, and the particular benefits that should be available to the personnel. *Such objectives constitute goals toward which the organization and each individual in it can direct effort.*

Procedures. Having established objectives or, in other words, made a drawing of what the completed job should look like, it is necessary to put the best possible thought into the development of a procedure required to accomplish the objectives. The mistake made by many administrators has been to outline to their organization what they expect to have accomplished and then to leave it to the individuals concerned to accomplish it as best they can. This, of course, is a broad-minded and fair attitude, but it does not provide those concerned with all the available knowledge and experience that would be of assistance to them in going about their tasks. Therefore, the administrator should exhaust every source until he has finally set up a *definite procedure representing the best thinking and experience in the organization* as to what should be done to bring about the desired results.

It is necessary to state that such procedures are not intended to be rigid rules from which no deviation may be made. What house was ever built without deviation from the blueprint? In the course of construction, partitions are changed, rooms are changed, many details are altered, but each change is made in relation to a basic plan and indicated on that plan. Working from a basic plan, we can be sure not to create chaos or greater difficulties when a change is made. In other words, *such procedures are starting points* from which initiative and ability will cause changes and improvements, each time making such progress a matter of historical record for the future guidance of others.

Assignment of responsibilities. Having determined what steps should be followed in order to accomplish the objectives, it is then essential to assign these steps to individuals as responsibilities. If this is not done, individuals, departments, or various units of the organization will be trying to do the complete job rather than certain important parts of it. The situation would be similar to the automobile plant, with every group of workers trying to make a complete automobile instead of each group working at an assembly line with a particular part of the automobile to make or assemble. In the first case, the finished product would be a matter of chance and there would be no uniformity as to style or quality; in the second case, all groups would be contributing to a finished product that meets desired specifications.

Planning versus Approval

A question just as old as, "Which came first, the hen or the eggs?" is the one, "How busy should an executive be?" There are those who believe that the proper executive atmosphere is that of long hours, missed lunches, batteries of telephones, last-minute traveling reservations, dictating machines by the bedside, and the like. There are others who say that the best executive is the one who never appears to be rushed or busy, who can do his work within the limits of office hours, who has the time to discuss anything with anybody, who delegates all responsibility, and who can occasionally play golf without fear of the business falling apart in his absence. Agreement on the answer to that question probably will never be reached because *management is largely a matter of personalities and not systems.* There probably is a medium ground between two viewpoints that comes more nearly to being correct than either of the extremes presented.

There are, however, some features of executive practice that seem to meet general approval. One is that the number of items or activities that a manager has to sign or approve can be greatly overdone. There are men who believe that a real executive job is sitting at a desk signing and approving. *The number of times a man has to sign his name does not indicate the extent of his authority.*

A principle that is fairly well accepted is that *authority should be delegated within definitely defined limits.* Some people do not delegate authority because they have not established limits for the control of authority, and each individual case has to be considered on its own merits. There are some managers, for example, who maintain that authority for salary changes cannot be delegated. Their feeling is that all salary changes should be approved by a salary committee or some executive of high standing. Such managers usually do not have any established salary group limits for each job—maximums and minimums—then it is a simple matter to delegate authority to any executive or to any supervisor to administer salary changes within those established limits.

These limits, within which authority can be granted, should be written into policy. The development of policy on a sound basis would build the road upon which we are to travel, and we would have the privilege of traveling on that road in any kind of vehicle and at any speed we care to, just as long as we stay on the road and reach our destination at the established time.

In other words, the better the administrative planning, the better the policies and the fewer executive approvals required. If management properly establishes objectives, procedures, and responsibilities in connection with the major activities of the operation, more time is available for further planning and greater perfection in present planning.

The complaint continues from many sources that executives and supervisors do not have time to do long-range planning because each day brings more than enough duties to fill the day. Somehow, sometime, we must neglect a day's duties, or get somebody else to do them, so as to have time to establish the course for tomorrow before the ship strikes a shoal.

CONTROLLING

Keeping in mind the two basic elements of management, planning and controlling, let us assume that planning has been taken care of through the establishment of written plans that outlined objectives, procedures required for reaching those objectives, and the assignment of steps of the procedures to individuals as functions. We then turn our attention to the element of controlling.

A study of many organizations of varied types discloses an unfavorable balance between planning and controlling. In some instances, there is a predominance of planning without sufficient control, and in other instances there is an excess of control because of the absence of planning.

It is most important, in considering this topic, to define what is meant by controlling. *Sound administrative practice sets up, in an organization, required media to insure understanding by all concerned of what is expected of them, provides sufficient help and information so that everyone is able to do what is expected of him, and establishes current indicators of what is going on.* Such media must also provide for the development of a desire to do what is supposed to be done. Controlling rightly implies proper supervision, which results in the elimination of many routine details that take valuable time away from supervisory activities.

Controlling does not imply centralization of authority. On the contrary, the best type of control is through decentralized authority. Controlling requires the delegation of responsibility and authority and the development of people who are able to accept both. Decentralization is most effective when there is centralized control.

Through misconception of what constitutes administrative control, tremendous duplication of effort and an abnormal amount of checking of others will be found in some organizations. Each stratum of the organization should be analyzed to discover the authority and responsibility at different executive levels.

Any manager or supervisor will greatly improve the effectiveness of his people if he will take the time to study carefully the construction of his organization and from such studies adapt his organization to the plans that have been made and to local conditions. If he will then give careful attention to the *quality and methods of supervision* throughout that organization, he can be fairly well assured that practically everything within his power is being done to direct individual and group performance toward established objectives.

Organization Structure

There seem to be at least two media of controlling. These are by no means all, but they are basic. The first is organization structure (Figure 3). This is a term that, like "policy formulation," has been used loosely, and yet it is a term that must be as clearly understood as "budget" or "personnel," or any other term that has a very specific meaning to us. Here is a definition from the experience of successful executives: *Organization structure is the control which makes it possible for individuals to work together in groups as effectively as they would work alone.* That is why we have organization structure. There is no other purpose for it.

If every person in an organization does not understand the organization, if there is not uniform visualization of it, if there is any confusion as to responsibility, authority, and interrelationships, the results are duplication of effort, omission of responsibility, friction, politics, jealousies, all of which create lost time and lost effort. It is very interesting, in attacking individual problem cases involving morale or personal relationships, to trace the organization structure concerned. You usually will find that the difficulty arises from misunderstanding or confusion as to individual responsibility, authority, and rela-

Figure 3

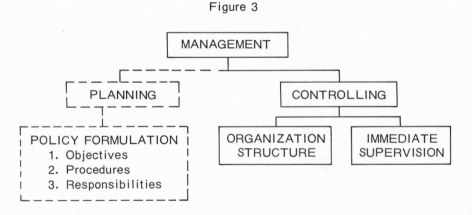

tionships with other people. *If an organization structure is not sound, the people in it cannot perform properly.* Successful administration requires simple, understandable organization structure.

These principles and observations seem so fundamentally sound that they are presented with some finality. Therefore, it is necessary to repeat that these are not the convictions of any one individual, but of many individuals with great experience and breadth of view.

An organization is an extension of the chief executive. He delegates what he wants, as he wants, and to whom he wishes. While he has an ideal organization structure toward which all personnel moves should be made, he has a current structure that .must be adapted to the competency of the employees available and the degree of confidence he has in those employees. Organization structure should be constantly changing and a subject of continuing study.

The Catholic Church is famous for its skill in organizing. Its full-time workers are educated and trained in the structure. A military establishment is highly organized and its officers and troops are on the receiving end of considerable training and review of organization structure. You can say the same about athletics. Why, then, do we neglect organization clarification in other segments of our society?

If we were still using the flying wedge as the best football formation, there would not be much interest in football. Along came outstanding coaches, however, who introduced the single wedge, the double wing, the T-formation, the I-formation, the lonely end, the blitzkrieg, the shotgun. Alert coaches are developing new formations, and they sometimes use several during a game.

Coaches cannot do this without spending hours and days in chalk talks and skull practice with the players. The players have to know the organization structure and the part each plays in it. Let each manager search his own soul. How much time have you spent in the last 12 months discussing organization structure with your team? How in the world can you expect it to operate as a team if you do not work at it? Team play just doesn't happen.

Because most of us have learned organization structure from our military experience, we are trying to inflict military organization upon civilian activities, and it doesn't work very well. Any manager who copies an organization structure out of a book is not fulfilling his professional responsibility.

Immediate Supervision

A second medium of controlling is immediate supervision. One of the trends of the times is that supervision is taking on new life, new significance, and deeper meaning. The time is here when the position and importance of supervisors in an organization are being recognized. Executives and administrators are realizing that supervision is a tool of management that needs constant sharpening.

Probably you have seen on meeting programs of trade and professional associations such subjects as "The Part of the Supervisor in Policy Formation," "The Relationships of the Supervisor to the Line Management," "The Supervisor's Responsibility toward Management," etc. It is gradually dawning upon us that the supervisor is not part of management; he is not a representative of management; he is not a liaison between worker and management—he *is* management. The president of a company may have 5,000 people under his direction, while a supervisor may have only 15, but the supervisor must secure from the 15 what the head of the company is trying to secure from 5,000. The head of an organization may have 30 basic activities with which he is dealing; the supervisor may have only 7, but the supervisor has to administer the 7 activities so as to produce the results that the head of the organization is trying to produce from 30. The head of a unit may have the world for his territory; the supervisor may have the corner of an office, but in that corner of that office, he is the boss and until we fully appreciate that, some of the human relationships we desire are not possible.

It is tragic when you hear some worker say, "I like my supervisor. Bill is a swell guy, but why should I go to him with my problem? He can't do anything about it. He has no authority. All he does is take my problem to someone else. By the time it has gone through three or four months or over three or four desks, it is so mixed up that everybody wonders what is the matter with me. Therefore, I would rather go direct to the individual who can settle my difficulty." Wherever such an attitude is present, full appreciation of the value of supervision does not exist on the part of management. *It is a challenge to management to answer whether the immediate supervisors of the workers should be encouraged and allowed to develop relationships with those workers that are based upon confidence and respect.* If the answer is yes, the supervisors must be given authority and must be trained to use it intelligently.

Somewhere in the United States right now, the following is taking place. A general foreman is talking with Harry. "Harry, you know that your foreman, Pete, is retiring this week. He has been with us 37 years and he is 66 years old. Friday night, we are giving him a retirement dinner, a watch, his first pension check, and wishing him Godspeed.

"You, Harry, have been with us quite a while. You are loyal, faithful, and can get more out of that machine of yours than anybody else. You can tear it down and put it back together again. You have made modifications the manufacturer never thought of. I would like, Harry, to announce Friday night that you are going to be the new foreman."

Harry's chest comes out, his chin goes up as he runs to the telephone to call his wife. She gets out his new blue suit and his Sunday tie; Friday night, he is congratulated at the banquet for his new responsibility. Monday morning, some thoughtful young lady puts a rose on his desk, and now he's a manager!

Doesn't that make your ulcers jump? Absolutely unprepared to be a manager! He knows nothing about cost control, waste control, or quality control. He does not know the company policies he will have to administer.

He doesn't know how to select a man for a job, train him for a job, introduce him to the job, or pay him for a job well done. He doesn't know how to handle employee grievances or deal with the union steward. A year from now, you have a multimillion-dollar strike because of some "dumb" action the foreman took.

THE EXECUTIVE FUNCTION

This presentation on basic principles can be summed up in this way. An executive, or manager, whichever you wish to call him, is supposed to:

1. Determine what he wants people to do.
2. Select and train as qualified people as he can to do it.
3. Check periodically to see how well they are doing it.
4. See that methods are found by which they can do better.
5. Discipline them. (Discipline has two aspects to it: reward for work well done and appropriate treatment for failure.)

Anything else that a manager is doing is not management.

II

General Management

SEVERAL BROAD PRINCIPLES of management cannot be easily categorized into the planning, organizing, and control model of management that is the major theme of this book. This chapter discusses these broad principles in terms that are familiar to educators because many of these concepts have been used for years in the field of educational administration. Most of these principles describe the actions and behaviors of people when they are part of an organization. They are based not only on sound psychological concepts but also on the empirical evidence gathered by managers in both the education and the corporate world. The detailed description of the planning, organizing, and control model of management will build on the broad concepts discussed in this chapter. The management concepts directly related to planning, organizing, and control will be dealt with in later chapters.

BASIC ASSUMPTIONS OF MANAGEMENT

Before management behavior can be studied, classified, analyzed, and improved, certain assumptions about the organization and its environment are necessary. The following assumptions are statements of the minimum conditions that should exist if professional management is to improve the performance of an organization. The degree to which any of the assumptions, or requirements, are not fulfilled indicates the degree to which professional management practices will be operating under a handicap. That being the case, professional management practices cannot be expected to improve the performance of the organization to the extent *theoretically* possible.

1. *A rational environment.* Decision making is the key function of all managers. It is therefore imperative that the environment in which the organization finds itself does not inhibit the decision-making process. If the organization is in an irrational environment, the decision-making function is not readily amenable to study and analysis because the decisions are ad hoc, tend to be random, and are often chaotic in the extreme. In this environment, one decision is usually as good as any as long as they are made on a timely basis. The leaders can react to and control crisis, but they cannot prevent it.

This is not to say that there must be total rationality in the world of education before professional management can be an effective tool for the educator. It is recognized that in most decisions political and emotional considerations are generously mixed with rationality. It does mean, however, that rationality should be maximized whenever possible and the rational elements of the environment must be cultivated by the educational manager.

2. *A clear concept of the institution.* If the manager is to succeed in achieving the goals of his organization, he must have a complete understanding of that organization. This concept includes not only the organization but also its relationships with support systems such as the school board, students, and other personnel within the institution; namely, teachers and administrators. Each component of the organization must clearly understand its relationship to the total organization and to all other components. If this understanding does not exist, the manager will find it necessary to frequently redefine basic relationships in light of the pressures and demands of the interfacing components. The constantly shifting relationships in the organization will prevent its maximum effectiveness.

3. *An accurate definition of the role of the chief executive officer.* Before professional management practices can be effectively applied, a precise definition of the chief executive officer's role must be agreed on by the individual and his board. His exact responsibilities and authority in regard to policy, budget, law, and organizational plan must be clearly prescribed so that conflict and ambiguity will not compromise his decision-making ability. Vaguely outlined responsibilities tend to limit his creativity and range of alternative strategies for achieving the goals of the organization.

4. *An appropriate self-concept of the chief executive officer.* The *self-concept* of the chief executive officer must be consistent with the role he has accepted from his board. Any significant difference between the

perceived role and the role defined by the governing board will decrease organizational effectiveness. The chief executive officer may suffer personal frustration as well as professional ineffectiveness if the difference between reality and perception becomes too wide.

Some school superintendents, as well as principals, view their role primarily as serving as a buffer between the school system, or individual school, and the community. Others view their role as working closely with the internal mechanism of the organization to insure that it operates with maximum effectiveness. Although the roles can be characterized as being at opposite ends of a continuum, both can be effective as long as the chief executive officer understands his role and does not make decisions that could be made by others who have more appropriate information. The chief executive officer should view himself as the person with the necessary responsibility and authority to see that there is a plan for the organization and that it is accomplished. The management skills and tools discussed in later chapters will assist the educational chief executive officer in developing an appropriate self-image.

5. *A concept of a management system.* If professional management is to be effective in an organization, the concept of management held by its leaders must be understood and shared throughout the organization. This concept should include an understanding of how the parts of the system function and an intimate knowledge of the boundaries between the various segments of the organization. The understanding of the interfaces between the segments of the organization should include the boundaries between strategies and action plans as well as physical organizational units.

Each staff member should understand the type of management system that operates within the organization. It is less important to determine whether the management style is highly participatory or autocratic or something between these two extremes than it is to insure that everyone knows what the style is and understands how it works. School systems can tolerate widely varying leadership styles as long as the behavior of the leaders is consistent and is accepted by other members of the school system. Management effectiveness is seriously compromised when the leadership styles are not accepted by other members of the organization or when the styles of leadership vary widely among the managers of the school system.

THE DECISION-MAKING PROCESS

The single most important characteristic of a well-managed organization is a clearly understood decision-making process. The procedure must be visible to all members of the organization as well as to its audience outside the organization. If the students, teachers, or other administrators do not understand how decisions are made in the school system, the managerial effectiveness of that system will be seriously impaired. Frequently, manifestations of this problem are labor turmoil, student unrest, poor staff morale, high personnel turnover, and public dissatisfaction with the effectiveness of the school system. Depending both on the public awareness of the school system's functioning and on the leadership style of the superintendent, visibility of the decision-making process frequently is more important than whether the process is democratic or autocratic. Most decision-making procedures are somewhere near the middle of the continuum.

Fortunately the authoritarian decision-making process has gone out of style. The days of an omnipotent dictator, albeit a benevolent dictator, have long since passed from the educational scene.

In contrast, a completely democratic decision-making system in the educational community too often has meant abdication of decision-making responsibility, with the result that no decisions are made. To work effectively, the decision-making process must be capable of delivering decisions when they are needed. If decisions are unnecessarily delayed, advocates of different viewpoints find their positions more comfortable and will become hardened in those views. They will more strongly resist any decision that does not agree with their position. A morale problem has been defined as the conflict between a personal decision long nurtured and a management decision long delayed. The most effective decision-making style in our present social context is participatory democracy. When this decision-making procedure is used, all segments of the organization affected by the decision have an opportunity for input. However, one person or a small group of people must be held responsible and ultimately accountable for the decision.

MANAGEMENT IS A WAY OF LIFE

Management is not an activity that is carried out to resolve problems or to accomplish certain tasks. Management skills are applicable to every facet of the manager's job. To be effective, the skills should not be used for management team meetings and public display. Just as good manners should be used in day-to-day family relationships as well as when guests are present, professional management practices should be continually used in the day-to-day activities of the manager.

It has been pointed out elsewhere in this chapter that if managers are to achieve maximum effectiveness, they must strive for a consistent pattern of behavior. The decision-making style should not fluctuate between authoritarian and democratic. General management practices and leadership style should remain relatively constant so that the energy of the organization can be used to achieve its goals and not be dissipated by working to overcome management inconsistencies.

Management is a way of life that is applicable to every type of organized endeavor, including personal and family life. The broad principles of management, as well as the skills and techniques of planning, organizing, and controlling, can be used with appropriate modifications to help improve the effectiveness of every type of organization. Every educational administrator is involved in civic, religious, professional, and cultural activities that are in need of improved effectiveness. The only change necessary to apply the principles discussed in this book to other organizations is a change to appropriate vocabulary and semantic patterns.

By using professional management practices in organizations other than the school system, the educational manager will have an opportunity to practice his skills in management and to sharpen the conceptual framework for his own professional development. Whenever inefficiency and ineffectiveness are allowed to become common in the operation of our social institutions, all society suffers. If our churches, hospitals, social clubs, civic clubs, professional organizations, and other organizations can become more efficient and effective, the quality of our society will be improved.

Very few of us enjoy the luxury of having infinite resources at our disposal. Whatever can be done to maximize the effectiveness of the resources we do have enhances not only the individual but the society in which he lives. Whenever inefficiency and ineffectiveness prevail in a social system, all those who are affected by the system suffer.

MANAGEMENT IS PEOPLE-TO-PEOPLE RELATIONS

The primary concept on which this book is based is that management is the art of getting things done through other people. The key to effective management is people-to-people relations, which is implicit in the definition of management. To be effective, a manager must be able to understand and to effectively deal with human relations. It is beyond the scope of this book to provide the educational manager with a list of steps to become more effective in interpersonal relations. Research studies and writings in the field of interpersonal relations, especially the developments in the field of sensitivity training in the past few years, offer a wealth of information on this subject. A few of the broad concepts of human relations and their application to management will be discussed, however, to provide a framework for the remainder of the book.

The keystone of interpersonal relations in management is an open, honest attitude. The old adage that honesty pays has never been more apropos than it is in the interpersonal relations necessary in management. If an organization is to maximize its effectiveness, every member of the organization must understand his relationship to the organization and to the other people that make up the organization. Each person must have an accurate conception of what is expected of him and a clear understanding of his contribution to the mission and objectives of the organization.

One of the more subtle but powerful outcomes of effective people-to-people relations is that each person has an opportunity for personal success within the organization. Given a careful description of what is to be accomplished and a mechanism to let him know whether the job has been satisfactorily completed, the person has an opportunity to succeed. Too often in educational systems people have worked for years without being able to determine if they have been effective in their professional lives. By having an opportunity for success, each person is given means for ego-fulfillment, as well as encouragement to succeed in the future. One of the tenets of education is that it is hard to overemphasize the motivational power of success. This concept is just as basic in management as it is in instructional programs.

The next article describes some of the problems met when planning is implemented in profit-oriented organizations. Almost all the author's comments are applicable to management improvement in education. The section on how to get started describes several concerns of special interest to educational managers. One of the most important is that planning cannot be delegated down into the organization. It must be the responsibility of a key man in the organization, a person who probably is already overworked.

Why Aren't Companies Doing a Better Job of Planning?

PATRICK H. IRWIN

Partner and Director of Planning Services
Urwick, Currie and Partners, Ltd.
Montreal, Que.

THE PILOT OF a jet airliner that had been airborne for several hours reported to his passengers over the public-address system, "Ladies and gentlemen, I've got good news and bad news. First, the bad news: We're lost! Now for the good news: We're making damn good time!"

Many companies are run this way—they're making damn good time, but they don't know where they're going. So, to chart the company's future course, they set up a planning function, which promptly falls into the same trap—it makes good time but produces little of real value.

Most managers agree that planning is a good thing, and many companies have established a planning function of sorts and, in fact, do some planning. But, to my knowledge, fewer than one company in 20 has succeeded in instituting a well-developed system of long-range strategic and operational planning.

Before examining why this is so, however, let us first review the need for planning and the planning process.

THE NAME OF THE GAME IS CHANGE

Every manager is aware of the immense changes that have influenced his company and his way of life during the past 10 to 20

Reprinted from *Management Review*, November 1971.

years and how future changes can dramatically affect his business. The way he runs his company must reflect shifts in people's attitudes on such subjects as work, leisure, knowledge, obsolescence, poverty, and pollution.

A company's survival depends not merely on taking advantage of technological advances when they become known but also on making an organized effort to explore and evaluate opportunities that are made available by new concepts and markets. For a company to remain alive—let alone improve its profitability—it must have managers who can forecast the major economic and technological changes that are likely to affect business, examine alternative courses of action and make intelligent choices among them, and convert plans into manageable actions that are designed to attain selected goals.

Meeting these requirements is what business planning is all about. It is an organized approach to managing a business profitably in a dynamic environment.

There are four phases in the planning process:

1. Business assessment—determining the company's position and opportunities and the threats it faces.
2. Strategic planning—setting goals, establishing priorities, and developing strategies.
3. Operational planning—making plans for each business function or activity.
4. Annual planning and action—insuring that plans are carried out by managers who are assigned responsibility for specific activities.

Most companies do a reasonably good job of Phase 4—annual planning and action. However, it is surprising how many still do not practice budgetary control or establish objectives for individual managers.

There are four basic reasons why a better job of planning isn't being done:

1. Difficulties in getting started.
2. Insufficient understanding of the present business.
3. Lack of understanding of strategy.
4. Failure to provide a system that integrates the goals of the company with those of individual managers.

GETTING STARTED

The first difficulty in launching a planning program can be getting started. Therefore, here are seven pointers on introducing business planning in a company.

Decide why you need planning, then commit yourself. There is no point in a company's launching a planning program unless its decision makers are convinced that there is a need for it. Top management must feel a sense of real urgency and believe that planning will help its company.

Don't start planning unless there is an effective decision-making process. Some managements are not accustomed to making long-range operational decisions, let alone deciding on strategic issues. Rather, they react to events. However, the end result of planning must be to make decisions on the company's future activities and the allocation of resources—money, manpower, and plant—to achieve defined objectives.

If there is no decision-making hierarchy or authority structure capable of approving plans and seeing that they are carried out, there is no point in beginning long-range planning.

Appoint a planning officer who is "someone who can't be spared." So that the work can be coordinated, a planning officer is required on a full- or part-time basis. He should be a highly competent manager who has the respect of the key decision makers. The fact that he usually will be someone who is already entrusted with heavy responsibilities elsewhere will put the company's support of planning to the test. If it really believes that planning is vital, it will not settle for a second-stringer but will appoint a man who is indispensable, or do the job with external help.

Make a plan for planning. Many planning systems have failed because the planners have not practiced what they preached; they have worked without a plan that defined the task and set dates for the work's completion. A good first step, therefore, is to assess the status of planning within the company and determine what end result is wanted, what work is required, who should do the work, and how long it should take.

Design a planning system. To begin to plan without first creating a planning system is to invite failure. The system should delineate the levels of planning, the channels and flow of information needed to formulate plans, and the process for reviewing and approving plans. The system also should cover the functions of those individuals and groups involved in the planning process—for example, the president, the planning committee, and the planning officer.

Get managers involved from the beginning. Assigning managers projects to undertake as part of the business assessment phase of the planning process will give them a better knowledge of the entire business and also give top management better insight into their analytical ability. Letting managers participate in the development of objectives, evaluation of alternatives, and strategy planning also is a wonderful means of developing management potential and a great way to achieve unity of purpose.

Don't attempt too much. The first long-range plan should be completed within 12 months. To ask for more time will risk loss of top management's support. Moreover, because it will take three annual cycles to get the system to work reasonably well, management should be modest in its aims the first time around, but should do the job properly and get it done on time.

INSUFFICIENT UNDERSTANDING
OF THE PRESENT BUSINESS

If you are going to make reasonable planning decisions, you must have a bedrock of sound facts and reasonable forecasts with which to work.

All too often, companies have foundered because their schemes have been based too much on visions of grandeur and too little on the realities of their performances and prospects.

Assessing a company's position, though, can be tricky. It is dangerous to assume that you already know where your company stands and what its strengths and weaknesses are. A company, for example, may not have all the information that is available on market or product profitability. Or, information that everyone thinks is accurate may prove to be incorrect because the coding system was changed a few years ago without anyone's realizing it. Then there are the skeletons in the closet that nobody wants to reveal.

What is needed is the unvarnished truth, even though some of it may be difficult to accept, and probably is unpleasant.

In addition to assessing its company's position, management also must develop a real awareness of the extent to which our society and values are changing, and, from this, assess their likely impact on business. Articles by economists, sociologists, and educators in business periodicals are useful sources of information, but contacts outside the usual business circles are needed as well.

Observers of society such as artists and poets—even science-fiction writers—should not be overlooked. They all are trying to interpret what is happening with people today, and their avant-garde thinking can sometimes provide clues as to what is likely to happen in the future.

DETERMINING ALTERNATIVES AND STRATEGY

Another problem in developing strategy is that most managers are not accustomed to thinking in strategic terms. When they are asked to plan, they frequently extrapolate historical trends into the future. This is probably because for years managers have been taught to concentrate on efficiency—doing things right—rather than on effectiveness—deciding on the right things to do. The result is that a good deal of planning is confined to those things with which managers feel most confident—for example, selling present products in present markets.

Unfortunately, managers too often plan on preserving the status quo, not in seeking change. All too often, they settle for objectives that are either expressions endorsing motherhood or goals for doing better what is done now.

It also is surprising how many managers believe that there are no available alternatives to the present activities and ways of doing business. To be meaningful, however, strategy must involve deliberate decisions to allocate resources in pursuit of the best alternative courses of action—bearing in mind the risks and rewards. And there are always alternatives—for example:

- To be a leader or follower in such areas as technology, product introduction, and pricing.
- To concentrate on further penetration of present markets or to explore new market areas.

- To sell in lower quality and higher volume or vice versa.
- To enter a new market through internal expansion or through acquisition.

INTEGRATING THE COMPANY PLAN WITH MANAGERS' OBJECTIVES

A fourth cause of difficulty in introducing effective planning is the failure to provide a system that integrates the objectives, strategy, and plans for the corporation with those of each manager.

Planning is useless unless managers take action. And the focus of their action should be on the vital things necessary to achieve corporate long-range objectives. Unfortunately, however, because of a breakdown in the communication process, managers frequently pursue the wrong goals or scatter their efforts aimlessly. This can be particularly true in the middle- and lower-management ranks.

The development of priority plans for each manager can be a valuable means of communicating company objectives and establishing the priorities and defining the results that each must achieve if overall goals are to be met.

As part of the operational planning process, each manager and his key subordinates will already have determined the critical areas where results are vital to the unit. This leads to the development of specific plans for year-by-year implementation. Priority planning with individual managers takes this process one stage further.

In priority planning, the manager and his superior sit down to review the manager's job in terms of its vital, profit-influencing elements. These tasks must be relatable to the division and company objectives. The manager and his boss then decide on the action to be taken and the results to be expected in the next 3 to 12 months; they describe the conditions that will exist when the results are satisfactorily achieved; and they note where the information to measure these results can be obtained. Finally, they identify any roadblocks that are likely to prevent the manager from meeting his goals and the actions to be taken to remove them.

Once the plan is agreed on, the manager is committed to achieving the results, and his superior to providing the resources they have settled on. At the end of the period covered by the priority plan, both will review the results that have been achieved, discuss causes for success and for failure, and set a new priority plan for the next period.

The management by objectives approach also should be linked to the identification of managerial training and development needs, salary structure and review, and succession planning.

The late Vince Lombardi, describing his success as a National League football coach, said, "We block, we tackle, we win. It's a matter of concentrating on fundamentals." Good planning demands the same: hard work, dedication, and concentration on fundamental issues.

III

Planning

WITHIN THE PAST DECADE, planning has been equated with motherhood and apple pie by many educators. The excellent reputation of planning as a critical factor in education is richly deserved. Planning is the keystone of management, and as such it should be the primary tool of the educational manager. It is the tool that enables the manager to accomplish the mission of his organization. In this chapter some basic concepts of planning introduced in previous chapters will be further developed by explanation and example.

Some writers have been able to trace the intellectual lineage of planning through the birth of the scientific method in the middle ages to the great teachers of Greece. The basic concepts of planning are similar to the basic steps of the scientific method. They are so similar that they suffer from at least one common problem: People tend to get involved in the form of planning and too frequently lose sight of their primary concern—the improvement of education.

Great effort is expended in attempting to define and then defend the various steps necessary to develop a plan. The planning process used by the American Management Associations at the Center for Planning and Implementation contains 13 to 16 steps, depending on the shades of definition given key elements of the process. No matter how many steps the planning process may have, three basic questions must be answered if the plans produced are to be of value: (1) Where is the school system at the present time? (2) Where does the school system want to go? (3) How is it going to get there? For a plan to be effective, either of the first two questions may be answered initially, but the third question cannot be answered until the first two are resolved. The clarity and accuracy of the answers to the three questions are far more important than the order in which the questions are answered.

Planning is more a state of mind than a series of intellectual or procedural hurdles. The simplicity of the three questions is not reflected in their application. The educator who is looking for a cookbook of planning success will search through mountains of paper only to find that his task has been fruitless.

SITUATION ANALYSIS

"Situation analysis" is a technical term for determining the present status of a school system in relation to a large number of variables. The analysis considers many different factors, such as the resources available to the school system, the present policies governing the organization, a statement of the beliefs and basic philosophies of the organization, an analysis of its major problems and weaknesses, a listing of its strengths, and an analysis of the organizational structure. This information is carefully considered in the planning process. A plan that results from the analysis will more accurately consider the actual capabilities and problems of the organization and will have a higher degree of probability of success. Without such analysis, plans tend to be unrealistic and ineffective.

OBJECTIVES

The second major step in the planning process is to determine where the school system wants to go. Without clear, concise statements of intended outcomes, it is impossible to effectively gather the resources and commitment necessary to achieve desired results. Objectives are a vital part of planning because, when they are communicated throughout the organization, everyone has a common view of the end result to be achieved. And if the commitment of individuals is to be enhanced, the objectives of the organization and of those responsible for meeting them must be as close to identical as possible.

In accordance with the complexity of the organization, objectives are usually stated in various levels of abstraction. They form a logical path that flows from philosophical statements to discrete objectives written in behavioral terms. The single most important objective is the statement of the organization's mission. This brief statement justifies the organization's right to exist and to consume resources. Earlier in history, the mission statement might have been chiseled in stone over the entrance to the organization's headquarters. Generally, this philosophical statement can never be accomplished. Here is an example of a mission statement of a local school system: "It is the mission of the XYZ School System to insure that every student leaving the school system will be capable of continuing his formal education or be capable of being successfully employed."

The flow of logic within a hierarchy of objectives eventually must arrive at a point of specific, behaviorally stated objectives. These specific objectives are sufficiently concise so that a single organizational unit within a school system can usually assume responsibility for their achievement. This example shows the quantitative nature of specific objectives: "By July 1, 1985, at least 50 percent of the students in Grade 4 will be reading at least the national norm as measured by the XYZ reading test."

The possibility of an organization's developing unwieldy numbers of objectives that dissipate its energy should be avoided. It is important that planning personnel consider specific objectives a useful tool in accomplishing the mission of the organization and not an exercise in trivia. Specific objectives are useful to help focus organizational effort. Excess numbers of specific objectives will diffuse results.

Depending on the complexity of a school system's mission, it may be necessary to develop a hierarchy of objectives, spelling out, at various levels, the details needed to translate the mission statement into specific objectives. Typically, only one intermediate level is needed to translate the lofty mission statement into the reality of specific objectives. The intermediate-level objectives are usually not stated in behavioral terms. Various names have been applied to the intermediate-level objectives, two of the more popular titles being "long-range goals" and "continuing objectives." More important than the name of the objective is its purpose. The objective should enable the personnel of the organization to translate the mission statement into action. Following is one example of a continuing objective: "Commensurate with his needs, abilities, and interests, each student will be able to function as an effective citizen."

The concept of objectives is comparatively easy to grasp. In practice objectives are not easy to develop into an integrated structure that represents the entity of the expected outcomes of an organization. The major deterrent is the difficulty in differentiating between ends and means. Because educators are typically action-oriented, they want to leap into action and immediately begin doing something. Too frequently, insufficient attention has been given to carefully defining the exact result desired. Planning then becomes an unproductive, frustrating administrative exercise in producing plans that gather dust and never will be implemented.

STRATEGIES

Many educators view strategies as the visible payoff point in planning. This is the segment of planning that describes what the organization will do to accomplish its objectives. Strategies are often viewed by the novice planner as the first real decisions made in the planning process. Careful reflection will usually confirm to the most impatient planner that decisions about objectives are of a higher level of magnitude than are decisions about strategies. The format of strategy statements is similar to that of objectives: "By July 1, 1985, at least 60 percent of the elementary school children in XYZ School System will be attending nongraded classes."

As many alternative strategies as possible should be considered during the planning process. There are many techniques of group dynamics designed to maximize the quantity and quality of ideas from a planning team. Extensive use should be made of these techniques to insure the highest quality of decisions for the school system. It is imperative that good management procedures result in more creative schemes for educating children, or serious questions must be considered about the efficacy of our general approach to the way we develop and provide education for our children.

As mentioned, the preceding example shows that the general structure of strategy statements is similar to the format of specific objectives. Strategies may also be described in a hierarchy that provides a variable level of exactness and impact. A broad strategy may describe an approach that will provide nongraded classes for a majority of the children, as stated in the example. A more precise and specific strategy would provide for the in-service education necessary to guarantee that the teaching staff will be successful in the new environment.

ACTION PLANS

A strategy is not a blueprint that can be immediately implemented. The detailed description of exactly what should be done and when is left to another segment of the planning process—action plans. Objectives, strategies, and action plans may be compared to a seed catalog. The pictures of the beautiful flowers or the succulent-looking vegetables are analogous to the objectives of a plan, in that both represent the desired result. The instructions that describe soil requirements, cultivation conditions, and length of growing season may be compared to a strategy. The seed catalog usually omits the action plan, the details of preparing the soil, planting, cultivating, spraying, and harvesting.

Short-range planning implies a different type of action plan than does long-range planning. This does not mean that implementation is ignored in long-range planning. The major difference is the obvious one, the time span; the secondary difference is the detail required by the action plans. It is important to keep in mind that the only plan that is influencing the organization is the one that is being implemented and that all other plans are history or an academic exercise. As was stated earlier in this chapter, planning is decision making; if no decisions are made, there is no planning.

The articles that follow have been selected to illustrate and augment the basic concepts of planning discussed in this book; they do not duplicate material presented in the past few paragraphs. Variations of the theme have been included to show possible alternatives useful to the educational planner.

Thorne Hacker, in the *Administrator's Notebook,* provides an enlightening discussion of the dangers and pitfalls in management by objectives as it applies to schools. He presents a detailed discussion of the key problem faced by most managers—the difficulty in obtaining the appropriate balance between trivial objectives and strategies and those that are so broad and vague as to be virtually useless. Hacker also discusses the problems present when management by objectives is applied to compensation. His discussion provides much food for thought as problems of personnel compensation continue to grow.

A dramatic appeal for planning in higher education is presented by Alvin C. Eurich. The same arguments that Mr. Eurich addresses to higher education can be applied to all levels of education. In addition to the plea for improved planning, Eurich presents a strategy of how planning can be implemented in an academic environment. The planning scheme he presents is a variation of the theme presented earlier in this chapter. All the elements of the plan and the process are consistent with those already described.

Staff functions, such as cafeteria, and school transportation, constitute one of the more troublesome oganizational areas in which to apply management techniques. Dale D. McConkey's article in the *S.A.M. Advanced Management Journal* describes techniques of using objectives for these organizational functions. Although the examples he uses are borrowed from industry, they are appropriate for most educational staff functions.

A lighthearted tongue-in-check article by Edward R. Bagley describes the pitfalls in planning. The problems outlined are applicable to education and will give the educational manager pause for considering his planning system.

A specific example of a planning process for curriculum development is provided by Richard V. Jones, Jr. in his article, "Tuning Up the Staff for Organizational Change." Although Jones does not directly describe his procedures in planning terms they do in fact offer a modification of the planning process discussed earlier in this section. The article shows how planning is used to effect a short-range, intensive change within a school system and also describes procedures useful in planning intensive activities such as Elementary and Secondary Education Act (ESEA) Title I projects and general curriculum development, in responding to specific problems.

The reader is urged to seek other articles from the professional literature of both education and management. In these few pages it is impossible to do more than capture the essence of the basic concepts of planning. The basic framework has been described. The reader must develop the details of his own planning procedures.

Management by Objectives for Schools

THORNE HACKER

Editor, Administrator's Notebook
Midwest Administration Center
University of Chicago
Chicago, Ill.

School officials are becoming increasingly concerned with the quality of services their systems provide. Desire to clarify and more effectively fulfill their mission has caused administrators to look beyond education for examples of practices able to focus objectives and integrate efforts toward their attainment. The attention of some large school systems has been drawn to the management by objectives (MBO) technology currently popular in business.[1]

Educators enjoy certain advantages in turning to an established set of practices. As borrowers, they are able to benefit from previous efforts at working the kinks out of MBO. On the other hand, they risk assuming that this technology comes to them trouble-free. To the contrary, MBO contains inherent tendencies creating pitfalls for the unwary and confronts the administrator with a number of difficult choices.

MBO has been described as an outgrowth of rational management theory as advocated by Frederick Taylor and his disciples. The technology's initial formulation is attributed to Peter Drucker, whose statement is contained in his 1954 publication, *The Practice of Management*. Its core features are relatively few. Management is guided by the specification of sets of objectives for positions within an organization. These goals are sufficiently concrete to

Reprinted from *Administrator's Notebook*, Midwest Administration Center, the University of Chicago, November 1971.

make their attainment evident. Thus the technology permits effective expenditure of resources and evaluation of individual performances in terms of goal attainment. Other elements have become attached to this core, representing choices to be made upon implementation rather than necessary parts of the package. Two options are participation of the employee in setting his own goals and an incentive system based upon payment by results.

INHERENT PROBLEMS

MBO programs typically measure performance exclusively in terms of goal attainment. The employee is considered to have performed well to the extent that he fulfills the objectives targeted for him. This emphasis upon hitting the target frequently results in the setting of trivial goals. Such objectives are especially likely to result when the program calls for goals to be negotiated by the employee and his superior. Under such conditions, it is patently irrational for the subordinate to maximize his risks by accepting challenging goals. His interests, instead, dictate a strategy of negotiating for easily attained and therefore, in all probability, insignificant objectives. Incentive to set challenging goals is lacking, for such objectives increase chances of failure when performance is judged solely by goal attainment.

Emphasis upon goal attainment also influences the kinds of goals that are set. The desire to determine readily whether a target has been hit results in the setting of easily quantified goals. For example, a principal may have as an objective an improved relationship with his faculty but for purposes of measurement, this goal is equated with the number of faculty meetings he holds during the year. In this fashion the concern for hitting the target results in the substitution of a trivial goal for a significant one.

Payment by results reinforces the tendency of MBO programs to produce trivial goals. The desire to incorporate an incentive system results in an emphasis upon goal attainment rather than broader criteria of success. Target hitting is an unequivocal criterion by which to judge what constitutes rewardable performance: The target objective has either been reached or it has not. Broader criteria of praiseworthy performance, on the other hand, lack this mechanical precision. The desire for complaint-free programs accounts for the frequency with which MBO plans incorporate target-hitting criteria and quantitative goals.

STEPS TOWARD SOLUTIONS

The tendency of MBO programs to produce trivial objectives can be partially counteracted by reducing emphasis on goal attainment. Basing performance appraisal on a variety of criteria, rather than solely upon hitting the target, frees the employee to experiment with more meaningful objectives. One additional criterion is the employee's ability to formulate goals that are both realistic and significant. Furthermore, taking into account the relative difficulties presented by various goals provides incentive to set challenging objectives. Another criterion is the effectiveness with which resources are employed in moving toward a goal regardless of whether it is attained. A major consideration is the employee's skill at analyzing those factors that intervene between planned and actual performance, for this capacity for intelligent review of past performance is the key to improved performance in the future. Attention to the entire process of setting and pursuing goals and of analyzing factors affecting progress toward them combats the myopia resulting from exclusive focus upon goal attainment. This broader perspective encompasses a wide range of skills and looks to the quality of goals rather than emphasizing attainment of a goal regardless of its worth.

The tendency toward trivial goals that results from setting easily quantified objectives can be checked through development of criteria reflecting worthwhile goals that cannot be easily quantified. The need is for instruments able to satisfy canons of objectivity without reducing high-quality goals to the trivial. Consider a case in which a principal's goal is to produce a system for managing student discipline capable of satisfying students and parents and of withstanding scrutiny by the courts. Attainment of this objective can be assessed in terms of the presence or absence of mechanisms contributing to an adequate due process procedure for students. Though the elements of an adequate procedure may vary with the school, a list of specific features might resemble the following:

1. The accused student shall be informed of the charges against him and of the evidence on which they are based.
2. He shall be permitted to testify in his own behalf and to call witnesses.
3. The appropriate administrator shall state to both the student and the complainant his evaluation of the facts of the case, his disposition of the incident, and the reasons for his decision.
4. The student shall be informed as to how his case can be appealed.[2]

Such criteria are one way to objectify performance appraisal without reducing standards to the easily quantified and often trivial components of an employee's behavior.

SIGNIFICANT GOALS

Reduced reliance upon easily quantified goals and reduced emphasis upon goal attainment open the way to serious consideration of worthwhile objectives; that is, objectives that are both significant and appropriate.

One criterion of significance can be stated as follows: The significance of an objective increases the more closely it approximates the organization's top-priority goals. Since the major goals of the entire organization provide the context that determines what is significant for that organization, they are necessary reference points for judging the worth of subordinate objectives within the organization. Objectives that contribute to fulfilling the oganization's major goals are more significant for the organization than objectives whose attainment contributes little to this end.

However, the application of this criterion is not trouble-free. Goals for the entire organization may be implicit or imprecisely formulated and therefore inadequately guide the setting of subordinate goals. Furthermore, even when these goals are clearly stated, the relative importance of subordinate objectives as related to top-priority goals may not be evident. For instance, in light of a school system's general goal of providing for the development of the whole child, how does one rank the relative significance of an expanded athletic program, hiring a school nurse, and employing an arts and crafts teacher? A third area of difficulty stems from shifting priorities among goals. Altered circumstances can result in goal shifts at the highest organizational levels or in adjustments of the relative capacities of subordinate objectives to contribute to the attainment of major goals. Either kind of change affects the relative significance of subordinate goals. For instance, a bond election required to finance an enriched instructional program may cause a successful athletic program or an attractive commencement to gain significance, for they become means of marshaling public support for the election.

As this criterion applies only to objectives subordinate to the goals of the entire organization, it leaves open the matter of how the significance of these overall goals can be judged. A reference point beyond the organization in its present state is required in order to judge the significance of such goals. The concept of progress, understood as the step by step approximation of an ideal state, provides a context for these judgments.[3] In these terms, an organizational goal is more significant the more closely it approximates that organization's ideal. This ideal need not be attainable; the notion of progress requires only that it be approximated more and more closely. The concept is analogous to a mathematical series, like: $1/2, 3/4, 7/8, 15/16, \ldots$; though each number is greater than its predecessor, the series will never reach its "limit," the number 1.

This second criterion of significance is a necessary adjunct to judging subordinate objectives through reference to the organization's top-priority goals. Without its application to overall organizational goals, reference to top-priority goals permits ranking of subordinate objectives but does not guarantee their ultimate worth. This guarantee requires a standard for assessing the significance of top-priority goals that incorporates an organizational ideal. In this way, the problem of significance becomes a matter of progress rather than maintenance.

APPROPRIATE OBJECTIVES

The fit between the set of objectives under consideration and other objectives within the organization constitutes one criterion of appropriateness. An organization embodies many sets of objectives forming a hierarchy running from the most general and often implicit goals of the entire organization to specific targets of individual members.[4] An appropriate set of objectives for a given position is one that is compatible with more general and more specific goals at higher and lower organization levels. In the case of a principal attempting to extract himself from a time-devouring commitment to an extremely small and phlegmatic PTA chapter simultaneously with the launching of a district-wide campaign to increase community involvement with schools, the principal's objective is inconsistent with a higher-level goal and is hence inappropriate. An appropriate objective in this case is kindling interest in the PTA by holding forth the promise of greater parental involvement in the school and using this group to fulfill this promise. By this criterion, a goal's appropriateness is increased in proportion to its degree of compatibility with goals at other organizational levels as judged on a continuum running from opposed to contributory, and in proportion to the number of levels taken into account.

A second criterion of appropriateness is the feasibility of goals in view of internal and external resources and constraints. An appropriate goal reflects awareness of the realities within an organization and is adjusted in light of available resources. The employee is one locus of crucial resources and constraints that often receive inadequate attention. The widespread business practice of employee participation in goal formulation and encouragement of candor between an employee and his superior help insure the availability of information sufficient to determine the feasibility of goals.

Additionally, feasibility depends upon factors beyond the organization capable of affecting the pursuit of goals. Some school MBO plans have incorporated mechanisms intended to guarantee consideration of external factors. The Chicago Performance Appraisal Plan, for example, stipulates that an administrator must involve community groups in the goal-setting process.[5]

Attention to present internal and external resources and constraints is, however, an inadequate basis for judging feasibility. Assessing the feasibility of objectives to be met in the future requires attention to emerging realities both within and beyond the organization. Without an orientation to the future, energy is expended on problems rather than opportunities and on yesterday's problems at that.

The question of whether objectives are best established for individuals or groups is an additional aspect of the problem of formulating appropriate goals. The prevailing tendency is to set goals for individuals; nonetheless, concern with integration of effort argues for group goals. The question, however, is not whether all objectives ought to be set for groups or for individuals, but how to determine which objectives are appropriate for groups and which for individuals. The demands made by goals and the capabilities of employees are primary considerations in making this determination. If pursuing a goal requires resources beyond those of an individual, then it is appropriate to set the goal for a group that has the required resources. When an individual's resources are sufficient to attain a goal, it may be appropriately set for him.

A glance at an elementary school principal's duties as they presently stand reveals that some are contingent upon the efforts of other staff members while some are solely his responsibility. Clearly he often operates within a power network, his performance relative to a particular goal depending upon the efforts of others.[6] His attempts to improve instruction are necessarily mediated by his teaching staff. His ability to supply his staff with desired materials depends upon resource decisions made beyond his school. Accordingly, goals related to instruction and the acquisition of supplies are appropriately set for groups. On the other hand, objectives concerned with classroom visitation and evaluation of teachers, chairing faculty meetings, and providing disciplinary support for his teachers are presently duties for which a principal is considered to have adequate resources, and hence are appropriately set for him alone.

The difficulties of establishing appropriate and significant objectives are many. Yet their presence serves to highlight rather than diminish the importance of developing workable criteria by which the worth of goals can be judged. Without these, any MBO program is doomed to become another paper-consuming routine, valued by no one and dispensed with in the shortest possible time.

PAYMENT BY RESULTS

A school administrator planning to implement an MBO program is confronted with the option of whether to link it with employee compensation. The primary reason for considering this alternative is the belief that such an arrangement will provide incentive for improved performance. This belief rests upon a number of assumptions. First, it assumes that employees operating within an MBO program need incentives beyond those integral to the program; that is, that the process of setting goals and judging performance by them (and the adjuncts of participatory goal formulation and appraisal, if these are part of the plan) are of themselves insufficient sources of motivation. This assumption requires scrutiny. Some evidence exists that target setting itself is the major influence upon improved performance while subordinate participation has a positive but less potent effect.[7] Further evidence shows that criticism disrupts rather than improves subsequent performance,[8] and the danger exists that failure to receive a performance-based raise will be perceived by the employee as tantamount to a highly critical assessment of his efforts. Consequently, refining the goal-setting and performance appraisal processes may be a more appropriate response to the problem of increasing motivation than a supplemental incentive system.

Second, tying performance to compensation assumes the universal attractiveness of a single kind of incentive and the efficacy of money as a motivating force. On the other hand, the ideal of providing the strongest possible incentive for *each* employee suggests an individualized approach. It is highly probable that a single kind of incentive is not the most effective for all employees, and even possible that money is a less powerful incentive than is generally supposed. The crucial question is, What kind of incentive is most effective for this particular employee? In all probability the answer will vary among employees.

The case for a plurality of incentives can also be argued from an organizational perspective.[9] Organizations typically have available a variety of potential rewards including promotions, approval from peers and superiors, increased responsibilities, and challenging assignments. Establishing an incentive system based upon a single kind of reward has the effect of impoverishing the organization's total range of rewards, for the reward offered by the system becomes the sole indication of managerial approval.

Should the decision be made to relate MBO and compensation, a number of troublesome questions arise. Are other traditional bases of salary determination, such as experience and training and the responsibilities a position carries, to be considered in addition to performance? If so, what is the relative influence of each? Should a performance-determined raise be in addition to a guaranteed annual increase, or should raises for a position be based upon performance alone? If so, are raises awarded for hitting the target or for exceeding it, or is the raise commensurate with the degree of success? If the latter alternative is chosen, how does one deal with targets, which by their nature do not permit gradation or cannot be exceeded? Is an employee penalized beyond the loss of a potential reward for falling short of his objectives? How is an employee with both individual and group goals to be rewarded? How large should a performance-based raise be to provide maximum incentive?

An adequate response to such problems requires that they be considered in terms of the impact of potential solutions upon motivation. As an example, the availability of rewards may be considered from this perspective. It is crucial to the effectiveness of an incentive system that employees feel increased effort will be rewarded. If the number that the system is able to reward is limited (that is, by factors other than performance), the character of the system parallels that of a zero-sum game.[10] This means that since the total number of rewards is fixed, if the number deserving rewards exceeds the number of rewards available, one employee is rewarded at the expense of another. This in itself has a negative impact upon collegiality and morale, and hence upon motivation. Furthermore, under such circumstances selection among the deserving of those to be rewarded typically relies upon some form of peer comparison, such as rewarding only those who exceed their goals by a certain margin. At this point, MBO abandons its distinctive focus upon individual performance, for this means of selection entails public reckoning of the relative worth of employees, those receiving rewards having been recognized as of more value than those who do not. Finally, the zero-sum aspects of the system weaken the connection between effort and reward, for the system is incapable of expanding its capacity to reward in response to an increased number of meritorious performances. Consequently, incentive to increase effort is reduced. In contrast, maximizing the motivational power of an incentive system requires that it be possible for all members of an organization to receive rewards should they deserve them.

CONCLUSION

A major pitfall accompanying any innovation stems from taking a narrow view of the ramifications of change. Unanticipated and undesirable effects can be expected from introducing MBO into a school system. A program of this magnitude will necessarily disturb existing alignments among delicately balanced elements of the school system. For instance, one would expect the program to have decided effects upon subordinate–superordinate relationships. Such a program cannot be left to run its own course. Means are needed of assessing how well it serves its intended purposes and at what cost to other components of the school system.

NOTES

1. The Chicago Board of Education has implemented a management by objectives program. See *Administrative Compensation Plan,* Board of Education, City of Chicago, March 1971.
2. The discussion of student discipline from which this example is drawn is Michael E. Manley-Casimir, "Student Discipline As Discretionary Justice," *Administrator's Notebook,* October 1971.
3. This formulation of progress is borrowed from C. West Churchman, *Challenge to Reason* (New York: McGraw-Hill, 1968), pp. 46–47.
4. Charles H. Granger, "The Hierarchy of Objectives," *Harvard Business Review,* May–June 1964, pp. 63–74.
5. *Administrative Compensation Plan,* March 1971, p. 9.
6. B. Frank White and Louis B. Barnes, "Power Networks in the Appraisal Process," *Harvard Business Review,* May–June 1967, pp. 101–109.
7. Herbert H. Meyer, Emanuel Kay, and John R. P. French, Jr., "Split Roles in Performance Appraisal," *Harvard Business Review,* January–February 1965, p. 127.
8. Ibid., p. 126.
9. Paul H. Thompson and Gene W. Dalton, "Performance Appraisal: Managers Beware," *Harvard Business Review,* January–February 1970, p. 154.
10. Ibid., p. 151–152.

*The key to survival is good planning. This means a
realistic look at where your institution is and the
setting of personal goals that are manageable.*

Plan or Perish

ALVIN C. EURICH

*President, Academy for Educational Development, Inc.
New York, N.Y.*

For most smaller institutions "Plan or Perish" is already a reality
today. If you doubt it, let me merely refer to the student unrest
on so many campuses, the dire financial crisis that confronts more
than 500 smaller colleges, the drastic problems facing such dis-
parate institutions as military schools, black colleges, woman's colleges, Catholic and other denominational colleges, and urban universities. In every one of these cases a crisis has developed because
goals are in contention, resources are unavailable, programs are
irrelevant.

Let's briefly pass in review the most critical problems facing colleges and universities today:

- Not enough money.
- Vague, not clearly defined objectives.
- Confused and hostile constituencies, including students, faculty,
  alumni, parents, and community groups.
- Anachronistic curricula.
- Outmoded and inefficient teaching techniques.
- Lack of enough top-quality teachers and administrators.
- Disagreement about the top priorities.
- Inefficient use of plant and facilities.

Will planning solve these problems? Not necessarily. It will if
it's good planning, it won't if it isn't. But the process of planning
is the process of addressing exactly these questions, and doing one's
best to answer them sensibly and systematically. One can bungle
the job, as in the case of the president whose administration can

Reprinted from *College and University Journal,* Summer 1970.

be characterized as moving from one crisis to the next; but unless one plans, the probability of success is slim indeed.

By and large, institutions of higher learning haven't even given it that old college try. Without outside pressures, few colleges and universities would ever change anything significantly.

And yet I think we are all agreed that changes—really significant changes—are needed in practically all institutions of higher learning. How can such changes come about? Planning is the rational, productive, and only feasible answer. It is the response of the intelligence to the emotional yearning for renewal that pervades higher education today. To be sure, every college and university must do some planning. For the most part this is done on an annual basis when next year's budget is being prepared. The kind of planning I refer to involves long-range projections.

COMPELLING REASONS FOR COLLEGE PLANNING

Some might argue that the rapid rate of change makes attempts to plan for the future foolhardy. I would argue just the opposite—that *the increased tempo of change makes it all the more necessary to plan*. Planning is a tool for dealing with rapid change, a way of coping with the unexpected.

A plan provides guidelines for measuring the validity of prior decisions. In the event of error, a sound plan, by offering these guidelines, increases the chances for corrective action before events run out of hand. In this sense, *planning slows down the onrushing future*.

A plan keeps the college on course. We all know that once a program or course of action is undertaken, it builds up a momentum and a constituency of its own and is painfully difficult to terminate. A plan, which has had the prior agreement of all concerned elements of the community, provides a built-in way of explaining and justifying the necessity of making difficult and often unpopular decisions.

However, I am not arguing that a plan must solidify the future. In some circumstances a plan keeps a college on course, in others it is a mechanism for changing that course if new conditions warrant it.

We must overcome the tendency to treat plans as static. Too many institutions undertake the Herculean task of preparing a plan only to rest back in the false assurance that the job has been done. Thereafter, whenever anyone asks where the institution is headed, the plan is taken off the shelf and leafed through. Such a procedure might have been suitable in quieter times. But today, events are moving so quickly that planning must be recognized as a continuing, corrective effort to maintain the fullest possible awareness and to take the fullest possible account of the constantly changing set of future probabilities.

In recognizing the need for planning, colleges and universities are only now getting around to what the better-managed businesses have done for years. Planning is tried and proven in business; in education, it is still an exciting frontier. But this lag suggests that we must turn to the task with alacrity. Time is short for getting higher education's house in order—that is the reason for the urgency in my title.

How Effective Planning Can Be Carried Out

The first essential step in planning is a *commitment* to plan by the president, the other key administrative officers, and the trustees. Without such commitment any plan that may emerge will merely be placed on a shelf and serve no useful purpose. The commitment of the president especially should be so strong that he pledges himself for a five-year period to carrying out the plan after it is agreed upon.

This procedure would get us away from all the fuzziness that now characterizes the trustees' and faculty's efforts to determine whether the president is really fulfilling his function. In business the evaluation of a chief executive officer is more precise; it is essentially the bottom line on a profit and loss sheet. Although we can't be that precise in judging the college or university president, we need to get his position out of the vague, indefinable area in which it has slumbered for too long. The precarious situation of higher education today demands no less.

Following the commitment, the next step is to *designate an administrative officer to be responsible for planning.* This officer in charge must make certain that all segments of the college community become involved in developing the plan—trustees, administration, faculty, students, alumni, and the local community. Not that the plan will be submitted for a vote by all groups—but all concerned groups should be heard before a plan is finally adopted.

Also to be carried on under the officer in charge is the *collection of all essential information* needed to formulate an adequate plan. If personnel are not available on the campus to do this task well, outsiders should be brought in to supplement the existing staff or to provide specialized services.

Finally, the major administrative officers under the direction of the president should *formulate specific, down-to-earth recommendations that are feasible and prepare a timetable* for carrying them out. These should then be submitted to the trustees for modification or approval, thereby obtaining a final commitment by all concerned to carry out the plan.

Characteristics of an Adequate Plan

Included among the essential elements of any adequate plan are the following.

1. *A description of the college as it now exists.* Often, these facts—covering characteristics of the student population; characteristics of the faculty such as salaries, education, and publications; the nature of the physical plant; and the state of the endowment—are readily available. *But the likelihood is that they have never before been systematically collected, codified, and analyzed.* Creating a plan forces a college to learn about itself, and this can be enormously enlightening. Hidden strengths and weaknesses are revealed, hitherto unknown facets of the operation are uncovered, and by the

time the compilation is completed, the officers and trustees of the college know their institution far better than before. In this compilation, platitudes and vague generalities are not and cannot be a substitute for realism.

2. *A clear statement of the goals of an institution that restricts its functions and does not promise to do all things for all students.* This in itself provides an extremely useful discipline for all members of the academic community. The job of any planning effort is to go beyond high-sounding and meaningless phrases and to arrive at a clear set of objectives for the specific institution involved. It should be directed toward a definitive statement of the particular kind of institution that the planners envision 10 to 25 years from now. Instead of the high-sounding generalities of the typical catalog, the statement should pinpoint the place of the institution in society, defined by its particular setting and orientations. It should identify its constituents, its character, its students, establish its particular emphasis on teaching, research, and service, or the balance among them, analyze its local community, and clarify relationships with the community and with other institutions.

3. *A set of assumptions for the future.* This also involves a valuable intellectual process. There are two kinds of assumptions about the nature of the future: internal assumptions, involving developments over which the college can exercise substantial control, and external assumptions, which include social and economic changes over which the college can exercise somewhat less control. The first group includes factors such as student enrollment, plant expansion, and faculty salaries. The second category includes developments such as rate of inflation, and extent of federal support. Here again, the very process of positing, researching, and formulating these assumptions forces the college to think deeply about the factors that will determine its future. The end product—the meshing of current descriptive data, goals, and assumptions about the future—will provide the college with a useful and meaningful plan.

4. *The projection of an educational program with methods for carrying it out and evaluating it regularly.* This program should state clearly:

- For whom it is provided—which involves a frank statement of the kind of students who are to be admitted and how they will be selected.
- The reasons for this particular kind of program. General? Professional? Preparation for graduate schools? And others.
- The breakdown by schools, divisions, departments, and courses with such difficult decisions as those on the size of the institution, enrollment by levels or programs, the faculty–student ratio, minimum number of students for any offering, methods of instruction, and kinds of experiences to be offered.
- Methods for evaluating effectively the instructional administrative personnel.
- Methods for evaluating student achievement and criteria for awarding degrees.
- Provisions for continuous improvement of the program.

- Special provisions for handling emergency situations as they arise, such as demands for black studies and other more relevant instruction, occupation of buildings by students, or other unexpected situations such as new government support programs, a capital gift of major size, among others.
- Procedures for continuous communication between the concerned groups as the plan is put into operation.

To be effective, the plan must also specify how the existing plant facilities are to be used and what new facilities are required to carry out the plan. This involves a projection of:

- The most extensive and economical possible use of existing facilities, including use during the summer.
- The best use of land owned by the college but not required for its educational purposes—such as leasing the land for additional income.
- Whether the college should own and operate dining and housing facilities—essentially hotel accommodations.
- New facilities to be built for the most effective and economical operation of the program.

Also the plan must project the people required to carry it out—administrators, faculty, and other support personnel. The hard question must be faced: Is the management capable of carrying out the plan?

5. *A statement of financial requirements to carry out the plan.* As a practical matter, we must bring processes of academic and fiscal planning *together.* Future program plans must be sorted out and costed out. When educational options are weighed, each option should have a price tag attached, and due consideration should be given to cutting back in some areas as well as advancing or expanding in others. A good part of the economic squeeze that afflicts colleges and universities comes not just from the limited amount of money they get but from the way they use those dollars. Proliferating courses and specialties, sacrosanct departmental fiefs, the size of the college, the penchant for small classes as an end in themselves, the aversion of technology, the reluctance to cooperate on an interinstitutional or an intrainstitutional basis, underutilization of the physical plant—all these contribute mightily to the cost–price squeeze (more important, they hold down the *quality* of learning).

6. *A provision for an adequate and regular accounting to the constituency of the college on how well or poorly the institution is doing in carrying out the plan.* This would include:

- The president's projections at the beginning of each year of what should be accomplished that year.
- An annual published report by the president of what has been accomplished. In this connection you will recall that even the philanthropic foundations have recommended this for themselves.
- A review of the president's effectiveness at the end of five or seven years as recommended by President Brewster of Yale.

SOMEONE MUST PLAN

It is clear now that unless institutions make their own plans, someone else will do the planning.

We are all familiar with the expanding federal commitment to higher learning. Federal dollars are, and will continue to be, most welcome to all of us concerned with improving the quality of our institutions. Federal support provides the opportunity for new buildings, curricular programs, and student aid, which we could otherwise not afford.

Yet along with the welcome dollars comes a tendency toward federal control. This is not unnatural since Washington, as it pours several billion dollars into higher education, certainly has a right to know how the money is spent. Yet federal control has its dangers. In its wake could come pressures toward standardized institutions, which do an injustice to the diversity of students and institutional needs in America. We must also fear the paralysis that could result from a massive higher education bureaucracy extending across the country.

The best way I know for colleges to avoid these dangers is for them to do their own planning, for them to vigorously begin to chart their own futures. Power flows into a vacuum, and if the colleges allow a vacuum of planning to develop we can be sure that someone will take advantage of it. But if colleges create sound plans, then they will be in a much stronger position to resist encroachments from the outside.

The staff manager must give considerable thought to his true mission in the organization before he can write worthwhile objectives. The failure of the staff manager to make this determination usually will result in his compiling a list of routine activities that he plans to pursue.

Writing Measurable Objectives for Staff Managers

DALE D. McCONKEY

*President
Dale D. McConkey Associates
Norwood, Mass.*

Pity the poor staff manager! So goes the thinking in many organizations. He deals in intangibles and he's there to provide service and advice to his line associates. Neither his mission nor his contributions can be measured. He's a complete nonentity in many instances—tolerated because of the occasional need for his specialized knowledge or an administrator of routine, ongoing activities—but often receiving neither the opportunity to make a profit-oriented contribution nor acceptance and recognition for his accomplishments when they are achieved.

Fortunately the "poor" staff manager need be pitied no longer. The advanced applications of management by objectives (MBO), or management by results, as it is often termed, now permit the staff manager to write measurable objectives, to measure rather finitely his contributions compared to his objectives, to receive deserved recognition in the process, and to take his proper place as a member of the profit-making team. Concurrently, the staff manager's organization receives value due for its money and begins to eliminate the management void that has existed since World War I.

This has been a most costly void and resulted from the failure to

Reprinted from *S.A.M. Advanced Management Journal,* January 1972.

measure staff managers and hold them accountable for achieving specific, profit-oriented results. The key to solving the problem lies in writing measurable objectives for those managers working in the so-called staff departments or functions of personnel and labor relations, public relations, finance, law, research and development, engineering, purchasing, marketing services, and industrial engineering.

WRITING MEASURABLE OBJECTIVES

The paramount difficulty in writing staff objectives is overcoming the long-practiced misconception that they cannot be measured—not in writing measurable objectives. Under MBO they can and must be measurable. To admit otherwise would be tantamount to agreeing that 20 to 40% of the average company's manpower budget is being expended on staff functions that can't be measured and that companies, therefore, must rely upon some form of divine guidance to make certain they are receiving value due for these tremendous expenditures. It should suffice to say that a company would be extremely reluctant to approve such amounts for any other type of project without first determining the rather finite measurements by which its return on investment would be gauged.

Take for example an organization whose "general and administrative expense" budget, exclusive of items such as interest on debt and other non-manpower items, approximates $2 million—a not uncommon situation. Further, assume that the percentage of staff costs of this figure is only 20%. Thus we are talking about a cost of $400,000 for the costs of staff managers and the matters for which they recommend, secure approval, and ultimately control. Now, this expenditure of $400,000 will be relabeled to change its cost classification and to illustrate the measures that would be required if it were, for example, a request for new equipment.

Before the company approves the expenditure, it would want to know, at the very minimum, the details of how, when, and for what the money would be used; the advantages of the new equipment over the old; the financial worth of these advantages; and the return on investment for the $400,000.

Assume a production manager walks into his boss's office and asks for $400,000 to buy new equipment; he tells his boss that it is impossible to determine or measure what return the organization will receive on its four-fifths of a million dollars of investment. The reader can image what would happen in his particular organization. In the first instance, no production manager worth his salt would ever make such a request. In the second instance, and in the unlikely event he did, his request would be turned down out of hand and his name would be moved to the bottom of the promotion list. If the company continued to retain him in employment, he would probably spend his next few weeks attending classes on basic business techniques for the student manager. Yet a company is guilty of exactly this when it approves the same expense for staff managers who have objectives or responsibilities that are considered incapable of being measured.

The indictment that staff objectives could not be measured was valid prior to MBO because prior to MBO these objectives, at best, were "for motherhood and against sin" types of objectives. They often read as follows:

1. To attain and maintain the highest possible degree of quality (for a quality control manager).
2. To provide expert financial and accounting advice (for a financial manager).
3. To design a product of the greatest consumer appeal at the lowest cost of production (for a design engineer).
4. To formulate and recommend programs that will promote employee interest and morale (for a personnel manager).
5. To purchase raw materials and supplies in accordance with specifications (for a purchasing manager).
6. To advise and counsel the company's managers in the preparation of both short- and long-range plans as an aid in achieving the company's objectives (for a planning manager).
7. To support the production department by providing well-thought-out recommendations on matters such as operational layout, work flow, and manufacturing processes (for an industrial engineering manager).
8. To enhance the company's image in the eyes of the buying public by securing the placement of publicity favorable to the company in media such as newspapers, magazines, radio, and television (for a public relations manager).

DETERMINING STAFF'S MISSION

The staff manager must give considerable thought to his true mission in the organization before he can write worthwhile objectives. The failure of the staff manager to make this determination usually will result in his compiling a list of routine activities that he plans to pursue. For example, the true mission of an advertising manager is not to formulate and administer advertising programs; his real job is to help generate sales by the type, manner, and cost of the advertising effort he completes. In similar fashion, the mission of the research manager is not to spend money carrying out research activities but to add to sales and profits by developing new products or improving old ones. An industrial engineer's job is not to conduct efficiency studies but to help increase production output. The major difference in all three of these examples is the distinct demarcation that must be established between merely pursuing activities and achieving specific results. Two examples will illustrate the importance of this difference for a staff engineering manager.

In the first example, the engineering manager considers his mission as being "to provide engineering services to the operating divisions." When he writes his so-called objectives, he will undoubtedly end up with a lengthy list of activities designed to carry out his mission; it would be all but impossible to arrive at any other type of objectives because he has cast his mission as an activity.

In the second example, the engineering manager states his mission in terms of the results he must achieve to justify his existence. His mission states that he is accountable for "effecting savings in plant and equipment costs through achieving X, Y, and Z results." An actual engineering objective covered by the second example reads as follows: "Reduce design engineering and manufacturing cost ratio to total equipment and rebuild cost from present 17.3% to 15% without reducing quality of design and manufacture of equipment."

Thus, before staff managers can consider writing meaningful, measurable objectives, they must arrive at an understanding of their true mission. Failure to do so will result in objectives that are not specific and not responsive to the real needs of the organization.

QUALITATIVE TO QUANTITATIVE OBJECTIVES

Prior to the extensive use of MBO it was usually believed, and practiced, that line managers should have quantitative objectives; i.e., those dealing with numbers such as sales figures, cost levels, ratios, return on investment, quotas, and profits. It was assumed, and widely practiced, that staff managers who dealt in intangibles could not have quantitative objectives but only qualitative ones in which the manager tried to state as specifically as possible that which he was going to accomplish. Even though it is still necessary for the staff manager to rely sometimes on specific, qualitative objectives, staff objectives are moving more and more to the quantified type. Following are two examples that illustrate the movement from qualitative to quantitative objectives. The first one is a general corporate objective; the second is a specific staff objective:

Example 1. Companies have long appreciated the value of having a quality reputation for their products. It builds customer confidence, sales, and profits. Thus companies frequently established an objective dealing with product quality. It usually read along the following lines: "Our objective is to achieve the number one quality reputation for our company within the industry."

At best, this was a qualitative type of objective and, while highly laudable, it could not be measured. No definition of quality had been agreed to and it was not possible to determine when or if the objective ever was reached. It was a "for motherhood" type of objective. Before it could become a meaningful objective in accordance with MBO, it was necessary to define what the objective meant and how it was to be measured.

The period of roughly the past eight years has seen organizations make dramatic strides in solving both the definition and measurement problems. This was accomplished by including in the objective *those specific conditions or indicators that must be met when in the judgment of management the objective has been satisfactorily accomplished.* With this technique, the preceding quality reputation objective is now restructured as follows:

"Our objective is to achieve the number one quality reputation for our company in the industry. This objective will be accomplished when:

"The number of field service calls does not exceed x percent.
"The in-plant reject rate is x percent or less.
"Warranty costs are less than x percent of sales.
"Labor and materials cost for rework does not exceed x percent.
"The company's product is rated in the first two positions for at least eight out of ten times in the monthly issues of *Consumer Highlight's* magazine."

This objective, which always was one of the most nebulous ones, now is a very specific one that can be measured quite readily. Managers know what must be done to accomplish the objective, and at the end of the target period they will know whether or not they have accomplished it.

Example 2. Now the same procedure, as illustrated in the preceding example, will be applied to a personnel manager's accountability for training and development. His mission is not "to conduct training and development programs," but to actually train a certain number of employees according to standards that will achieve certain specified results.

Prior to MBO, this manager's qualitative objective probably read: "To formulate and conduct training programs to insure the availability of trained personnel to meet the company's manpower requirements."

As was the case in the preceding example, this objective suffers from the lack of definition as to what was meant and some method of measuring whether or not it is accomplished. It moves from qualitative to quantitative status when it is restructured as follows:

"To meet manpower requirements of the company by formulating and conducting training programs that will achieve the following results:

"A replacement has been trained and is qualified for promotion for each job at Salary Level 15 or above.
"Three graduate mechanical engineers are capable of promotion to the senior level.
"Twelve foremen have completed and achieved a grade of 80 or better in the course 'Basic Supervisory Techniques for Foremen.'
"At least 4 stationery engineers have completed the necessary training and have secured the license for First Class.
"Twenty clerk–typist trainees have completed typing Course A and are able to type copy at the rate of at least 50 words per minute."

Here again, this objective illustrates how a general, qualitative one can be highly quantified and made into a meaningful, measurable objective. This procedure will be illustrated further with a few brief examples for other staff managers.

Credit manager. This manager's true mission is to generate increased sales through the manner in which he extends credit and collects accounts receivable. Both functions can exert a significant impact on profits. If he is too strict when approving credit, he can cost the company increased sales. On the other hand, a larger amount of bad debts may result if credit is extended too loosely. He can cost the company money that it could earn from interest if collections are not made on time. Thus the conditions he must meet, to adequately perform his job, might be spelled out as follows:

"The credit manager will have performed his job in a satisfactory manner when:

"Credit limits have been established for all accounts.

"Credit applications are approved or disapproved within two days of receipt in 98 percent of the cases.

"Accounts receivable are collected within 30 days for 60 percent of outstanding receivables and 45 days for 38 percent of receivables.

"Bad debts do not exceed 2 percent of sales for the year.

"No loss of sales results from the above."

Development engineering manager. The qualitative objective for this manager usually would dwell upon his responsibility for designing and developing products and processes. His true mission is to enhance profits by the manner in which he runs his function, and his profit contributing role is clear when spelled out as follows:

"The manager of development engineering will have performed satisfactorily when he achieves the following results. (*Many development projects require more than one year to reach fruition, and usually the objective covers more than the one-year period used in this illustration.*)

"Development costs are within a plus or minus 5 percent of budget for 98 percent of projects.

"At least three new products reach the commercial stage and each achieves the sales and returns specified by company policy.

"Savings of at least $50,000 are realized through the improvement of present products. These savings may result from reductions in labor, materials, or equipment.

"Move Project A to a position where a "go" or "no go" decision may be made by September 1."

In summary, often a staff objective can be changed from a qualitative type to a quantitative one by first deciding the specific result desired and then listing or describing the specific conditions that will have been met when management considers the requirements of the objective to be satisfied.

MAKING OBJECTIVES SPECIFIC

Although it is desirable to quantify staff objectives as much as it is prudent to do so, it is not always possible or prudent to insist upon complete quantification.

In terms of being prudent, it is more worthwhile to the company to approve an objective of considerable importance even though the objective can be quantified to a lesser degree than it is to approve an objective of lesser worth that can be quantified to a greater degree. Assume, for example, a financial manager having responsibility for financial forecasting and forms control. It is more difficult to quantify an objective covering financial forecasting than one covering forms control. If the company insists upon extensive quantification, the financial manager might be prone to recommend an objective, and a highly quantified one, that provides he will reduce the cost of printing forms by 5 percent. He doesn't recommend one for financial forecasting because it would be more difficult to structure.

The insistence on extensive quantification, in this example, has cost the company money because the savings from not printing forms may have equaled a few hundred dollars, while the loss through not pushing improved financial forecasting may have cost thousands of dollars or more. The same reasoning is applicable in the instance of a personnel manager who recommends an objective to reduce by x mills the unit cost of paper cups used in the cafeteria but doesn't recommend an objective covering a much-needed compensation plan because the latter is more difficult to quantify.

Nor it is always possible to completely quantify staff objectives. To insist upon complete quantification in those instances in which it is not possible will not result in better objectives; it will result in much wasted effort by staff managers as they try to do the impossible, and their faith and value in the MBO system will suffer. Like many facets of the management process, there are no clean-cut, ironclad rules as to the dividing line separating over-quantification from lack of quantification. This is a matter that each organization and its managers must decide. However, there are a few proven ground rules that, when followed, will help make any objective more specific in terms of definition and measurability.

Results, not activities. Staff managers can improve their objectives appreciably by wording the objective in terms of the result they plan to achieve rather than the activities in which they will engage. It is far better to describe results, even though the result itself may not be capable of one hundred percent accuracy in definition, than to talk about activities. Here are examples of both.

Activity	To conduct market research studies to improve the sale of company products.
Result	To select by July 1 three test markets for testing new Product B.

Who, what, and when. Another technique for making objectives more specific is to make certain there is a clear statement of what is going to be accomplished, who is going to accomplish it, and when it is going to be accomplished. These are the three salient points of any delegation and should certainly be included in the objectives of an MBO system, which essentially is a system for delegating the responsibility for results through all levels of management.

Avoid relative terms. There is a tendency, especially concerning staff objectives that cannot always be quantified completely, to lapse into the expediency of using relative terms to describe results. Words such as "adequate," "sufficient," and "reasonable" are poor substitutes for more descriptive ones; they lead to countless misunderstandings and make measuring practically impossible. Consider the word "sufficient." What does it mean? Does it mean the same to all people? Can the magnitude of results be measured? Is it a sufficient standard against which to reward or discipline a manager? Can it be used to prepare a financial plan?

All relative terms should be replaced with more precise ones even though the more precise words still may fall short of complete precision. For example, instead of using the relative word "reasonable," state the result within parameters. Even wide parameters are preferable to the relative word. Examples:

Poor	To achieve a *reasonable* improvement in the time required to prepare and distribute the monthly report of operations.
Better	To reduce by 5 to 15 percent the time required to prepare and distribute the monthly report of operations.
Poor	To effect as much reduction *as possible* in the cost of operating the law department.
Better	To reduce the cost of operating the law department by 10 to 30 percent.
Poor	To direct the quality assurance function in a manner *sufficient* to meet anticipated needs.
Better	To improve product quality by recommending inspection procedures designed to detect 80 percent of substandard products.

The reader will note that none of the alternatives listed under "better" are perfect; however, they are infinitely more valid objectives than the ones that included relative terminology.

Management by objectives provides the staff manager with the vehicle and opportunity of gaining acceptance of his function and recognition of his contributions. MBO provides the opportunity only. The degree to which the manager capitalizes on this opportunity depends in large part on how adept he becomes in structuring measurable objectives. To accomplish this, he must first determine what his true mission is within the organization (for what he is really accountable) and then translate this accountability into specific, realistic, and measurable objectives that play their proper role in achieving the objectives of all other departments and the overall objectives of the organization.

How to Avoid Glitches in Planning

EDWARD R. BAGLEY

President
Bagley and Co.
Wilmington, Del.

There comes a time when a manager must try out the corporate planning process that he's learned about at management seminars, business school, or the like. He says, or is told, "There must be a better way!" "Instead of letting the business run you, you should run the business!" or, "You've got to manage change, not be buried by it!"

It has been said that planning is like motherhood: Everyone is in favor of it—that is, everyone except those who never get to plan or who gum it up for themselves and for us. Almost everyone, though, at least pays lip service to corporate planning. Yet many companies, profit centers, and cost centers still don't have good plans or a good planning process.

The problem is that despite the enthusiasm for corporate planning, interest rarely lasts through the real planning process. What is needed, therefore, is some method that connects our ideas and enthusiasm to sounder performance and that fits our jobs, bosses, and problems.

In planning, there are five "glitches," as they are known in the electronics industry—unexpected failures of things that weren't supposed to fail. Each has a solution, and the solutions suggested here are proven planks for the bridge that will transport us to profitable performance in corporate planning.

1. *Unwillingness.* Despite an announced corporate commitment

Reprinted from *Management Review,* March 1972.

to planning, some executives who are responsible for planning simply do not want to plan.

2. *Lack of know-how.* Executives may be willing to plan or even interested in planning, but they may not know how to go about doing it, even after being taught the principles of planning.

3. *Absence of ground rules.* A company's executives may be willing and able to plan, but they can still be hampered by the lack of corporate data, guidelines, or policies.

4. *The possibility of ill-fitting plans.* Good individual plans cannot necessarily be synthesized into a performable corporate or divisional plan.

5. *Lack of support.* Both individual and corporate plans sometimes have to be aborted because of a lack of minimal supporting services.

GLITCH NO. 1: UNWILLINGNESS

The first glitch is very familiar and so frequently unsolved that it might seem easier to give up here without an effort. In fact, in some cases we may have to give up; there are some persons who cannot be led, chivvied, or forced into a "plan-ful" business life. In those cases we just have to plan without them.

However, excluding these hard-core "unplannables," there are several methods with which we can overcome the unwillingness to plan. Most of these incorporate participative management in some form.

In the case of a manufacturer of high-margin chemical products, the day-to-day demands on six key executives had delayed for more than a year the completion of even the first draft of a plan. Finally, outside help was enlisted—more to help get the planning done than to do it for the company.

Of the steps taken to solve this glitch, one of the most useful was a series of meetings in which all six executives and the president participated. After a silent beginning, first one manager and then another raised questions that had been inhibiting their planning attitudes. Fascination with the issues as well as some lively, healthy arguments—only occasionally interrupted by the planning consultant—developed.

The sessions became increasingly exciting—the kind of excitement that kindles people and their ideas. Other group sessions followed. Within less than three months, all but one of the six key managers had submitted a proposed plan.

The point here is not that the solution to unwillingness lies in group planning sessions. Rather, the point is that opportunity is available to unlock much of the classic unwillingness to plan among many, if not almost all, managers who are nominally responsible for planning. We shouldn't give up before we start because of our managers' unwillingness to plan. This often can be transformed at least into a journeyman grade of planning interest and performance.

GLITCH NO. 2: LACK OF KNOW-HOW

The failure of some managers to plan, although they are willing to do so, may stem from their lack of knowledge as to how to go about the task.

This is a common glitch, too. Most managers aren't born experts at planning, and usually no amount of general instruction or haranguing can explain planning sufficiently to transform willingness into intelligent effort.

The solution to this glitch usually does not lie in discussing the need for planning, nor is it found by considering our performance in planning as an important part of our evaluations or ratings for the year. Rather, the solution lies in step-by-step coaching in the use of a simple, common-sense approach to organizing business ideas and putting them on paper.

For example, the first time a New England metalworking company tried its planning system, it made several obvious mistakes. The manager of a recently acquired subsidiary in the aluminum storm door business, for instance, projected a pretax profit for the next year of nearly $1 million. The subsidiary's current annual sales amounted to only about $1 million. The manager wasn't trying to con anyone—he just didn't understand how to get from here to there in terms of corporate planning.

It took the New England company at least two full years of planning to teach its managers how to plan and to get some usable plans. To eliminate the lack-of-experience glitch that existed within the company, those managers who supported the planning effort:

- Provided specific critiques of the first plans. For example, management at the storm door subsidiary was helped to see why the subsidiary couldn't add $1 million in pretax profits in one year.
- Talked to, not at, the contributing managers, explaining to them the company's planning process.
- Shaped up corporate-level plans and planning, to give profit-center managers some better bases, to tighten the overall situation, and to set a better example. For instance, these managers devised an acquisition program at the corporate level and made plans to buy up some of the company's stock in the market at a cost well into seven figures.

With these and other "how to" aids to help its managers plan, as well as plenty of hard work, the company, which is in a nongrowth industry, in less than ten years more than doubled its sales, earnings, and earnings per share.

To solve the lack-of-experience glitch, it is evident that patient coaching is needed. This also may help solve some of the unwillingness to plan, which may stem from lack of knowledge. Unfortunately, some companies fail to see glitch No. 2 and consequently lose the planning battle because of a remediable lack of elementary planning know-how.

GLITCH NO. 3: ABSENCE OF GROUND RULES

Some willing and able planners may be asked by their companies to create plans without being given information on corporate parameters. For example, a proprietary drug and toiletries manufacturer that was stuck on a sales and profit plateau accepted a recommendation to begin planning for growth. However, it overlooked its planners' need for ground rules.

Ground rules for planning may include corporate objectives, company strategies, or planning assumptions. In this case, two of the several essentials that were not disclosed were the kinds of industries and product types that could be included in growth plans and the extent to which acquisitions could be planned as a part of the hoped-for growth.

On the question of industries and product types, the vice president of manufacturing, who also was a board member, was opposed to all new products that couldn't be made efficiently on the existing high-speed mixing and packaging equipment. On the other hand, the director of new products wanted to be free to add, say, lawn-care products to the present group of proprietary drugs and toiletries. In addition, the question of acquisitions found some board members in favor of putting the company's $2.5 million of surplus cash to work; others were convinced that the company should put its own house in order before trying to acquire other companies.

These differences were resolved only after painstaking work at the corporate level—work that hadn't been contemplated when the plans originally were called for. Some of this corporate homework resulted in the formulation of unexpected ground rules. For example, it was found that the surplus $2.5 million was already committed, and this and other considerations led to a several-year ruling against acquisitions.

By establishing planning guidelines as well as carrying out many other planning and managerial tasks, this once-small company has been able to grow over 800 percent in sales, earnings, and earnings per share. Solving glitch No. 3—the lack of planning ground rules—was only one step in the company's corporate planning process. However, it is evident that not even rough plans could have been prepared if ground rules had not been laid down first.

GLITCH NO. 4: THE POSSIBILITY OF ILL-FITTING PLANS

When planning is done by those managers who will be responsible for carrying out the plans, we can end up with a series of ill-fitting individual plans unless the plans are reviewed and revised so that the corporation and each of its profit centers end up with mutually supportive plans and operations.

One case in which the whole plan became less than its parts involved a rapidly growing service company with a roster of blue-chip clients. Because the various departmental plans had been approved individually by the chief executive, it only became apparent later—when the plans were in operation—that each of the department plans called for more performance from other departments than those departments possibly could provide. For example, the marketing group had been "planned" to provide over twice as much support as it could supply. More recruiting results than the personnel staff could handle also were called for.

Clearly, the solution was to add review stages to the planning process, so that foreseeable conflicts and contradictions could be resolved and changes made in individual plans before they became operational.

GLITCH NO. 5: LACK OF SUPPORT

It is true that the responsible executive should both design and execute his plan; the bright young M.B.A. shouldn't try to impose his planning solutions on division managers, heads of staff groups, or others on whose management the success of the business depends. However, even the most willing and most able manager/planner rarely has time to do personally all the planning for his profit or cost centers. The same is true of the people in his unit. A generally acceptable solution to this problem has been to let the manager/planner, supported as much as possible by his own people, do the essentials of the planning job. The balance of the planning work then is completed by internal or external support groups.

What happens, however, when the manager/planner and his helpers aren't suitably supported in the parts of the planning work that can be done by inside staff groups or by outside services? To illustrate what can happen, let's take the case of a diversified midwestern manufacturer of metal products, including oil field production equipment.

This company's equipment division, acquired a few years before, was a loser, although the division manager and his line superiors in the corporation had planned and planned in order to turn the business into a profitable operation. Most of the managers who did this planning were capable, as shown by the above-average success of the other company divisions.

The glitch? There wasn't enough time, knowledge, or experience at either the division or corporate headquarters to do all the needed planning. The solution was to (1) rearrange priorities and assign a large portion of the corporate vice president of marketing's time to the preparation of the first comprehensive plan for the division; (2) use corporate staff support that had been assigned previously to other projects; (3) assign, with top-priority status, the preparation of the comprehensive plan to the division manager; (4) provide outside counsel to help render an objective evaluation of previous plans and operations—with special attention to marketing research—and to handle some of the staff-type development work for the comprehensive plan.

This solution produced for the first time a plan that enabled the corporation and its division to build in a more "plan-ful" and sounder manner.

Tuning Up the Staff for Organizational Change

RICHARD V. JONES, JR.

Chairman, Department of Education
Stanislaus State College
Turlock, Calif.

Change in education, like apples at the market, comes in different shapes and sizes. Richard Miller has developed a helpful model of these differences as they affect the number of people involved and time needed to implement.[1]

The model of innovation types can be visualized as a continuum, which functions to delimit at least three major kinds of changes: methodological, instructional, and organizational (Figure 1).

As indicated, the amount of planning necessitated by these factors increases in direct proportion to the number of people involved and the time needed for implementation. The function of effective planning is the major concern of this paper.

Methodological changes, those in Area I of the chart, are innovations that individual teachers can implement within their own classrooms utilizing existing time, space, and group facilities. Examples would be inquiry training, small group procedures, and new approaches to reading, writing, or problem solving. The amount of planning is limited because the individual instructor is constantly in command of the situation. Should the new system begin to sputter or falter in any way, in the opinion of the teacher, a return to former methods can be quickly accomplished. In fact, these kinds of changes probably occur regularly in most school

Reprinted from *Journal of Secondary Education*, December 1969.

[1] Richard I. Miller, ed., *Perspectives on Educational Change* (New York: Appleton-Century-Crofts), 1967.

Figure 1. A model of innovation types.

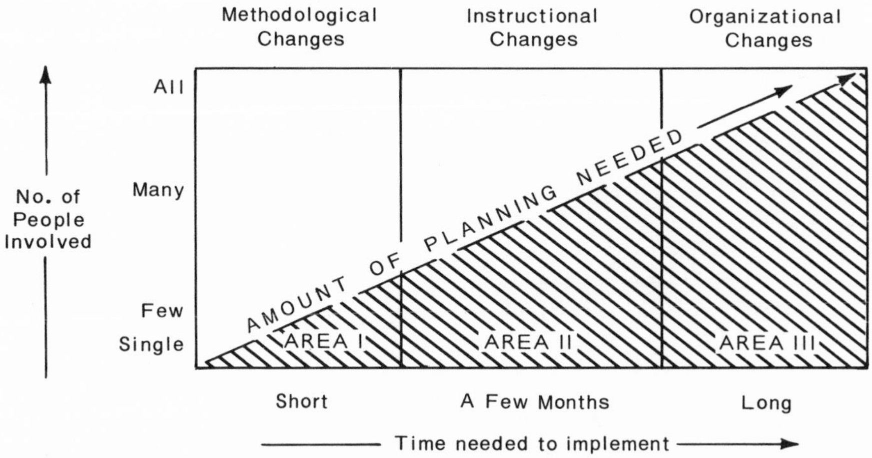

Adapted from Richard I. Miller, ed., *Perspectives on Educational Change* (New York: Appleton-Century-Crofts), 1967, p. 369.

systems where teachers are informed of specific teaching procedures through in-service training, or other teacher education programs and materials.

Instructional changes (Area II) include those innovations that involve more than a single staff member and involve some modification of time, space, student groups, or instructional materials. Examples would be shared or teamed teaching, implementation of any of the several curriculum studies (PSSC physics, BSCS biology, or ALM foreign language), the use of language labs or instructional television. If several teachers are planning to work together, or if a significantly large financial outlay is needed, broadly based discussions of policies, procedures, and practices are necessary. In addition, the return to previous systems is not as simple and direct as it is with methodological changes. Therefore, the critical nature of more long-range planning is apparent. Gordon Cawelti in *Nations Schools* notes that a high abandonment rate of innovations occurs in this area.[2] He indicates that the literature is unclear regarding the reasons for this "dropout phenomenon," but insists that careful planning prior to adoption seems related to most successful new programs.

Organizational changes (Area III) are the third major type of educational innovations. These are the innovations that include a general overhaul of the entire educational system. Examples would be a continuous progress program, flexible scheduling, staff differentiation programs, and other major renovations of the educational system. The Hughson Project falls into this category because it included not only the reorganization of the entire curriculum but also

[2] "Innovatative Practices in High Schools: Who Does What Why– and How," April 1967, n.p.

the development and implementation of new staffing patterns, new instructional procedures, new grading and clerical systems, and new skills by every professional at the school.

As the graph indicates, however, these change types are not mutually exclusive; they run together and overlap in a continuum. Continuous progress, as an organizational change, significantly affects both instructional procedures as well as methodological practices. This fact may help explain why organizational changes are the most difficult kinds of innovations to achieve and maintain in a school system. Organizational modifications are the basic changes, core changes that attack the interactive "face" between the student and that which he is to learn.

Charles H. Wilson, superintendent of North Orange County Junior College District, emphasized the need for such basic changes as follows:

> Innovation and experimentation in education have become respectable in recent years. A school without its team teaching, its ungraded classroom, its teaching machines, its open or closed circuit television is simply not with it. Even the public, long resistant to progressive education, and suspicious of change, today demands panaceas for what are widely believed to be the school failures.
>
> I have no quarrel with the current mood or with the innumerable proposals to overhaul the creaky machinery of mass education. But, by and large, we offered a flood of superficial band-aids for an internal sickness. We are attempting to modernize a vehicle designed for horse and buggy days with a patchwork of chrome.[3]

Organizational changes, the basic "organic" changes in education, are the types of changes that require the best-thought-out plans. The essential purpose of this paper is to suggest a series of steps that seem appropriate to any major organizational innovation.

Simply stated, these steps are:

1. The examination of present practices.
2. The clarification of purposes.
3. The examination of new models.
4. The development of new skills.
5. The protection of change.
6. The feedback for growth.

These steps will overlap, but each are vital to any significant change. They are listed with the assumption that the *standard* conditions for organizational change are operational. These standard conditions include at least these three: (1) an atmosphere of freedom that encourages thoughtful experimentation, (2) an organizational hierarchy that not only values competence but also

---

[3] Charles H. Wilson "Educational Innovation: Are Public Schools Going Overboard?" *Nations Schools*, November 1967, p. 66.

assumes competence in all staff members, and (3) an organization in which decisions are made as close to the operational level as is possible.

It is within this framework that each of the steps will be discussed.

EXAMINATION OF PRESENT PRACTICES

The detailed examination of present practices seems a productive first step before proceeding with something "new." Too often in education we jump to innovations only because they are innovative, not because of the evidenced failure of ongoing programs.

This initial examination involves more than a cursory overview. Inherent in this process would be the gathering, organizing, and analyzing of some rather specific data related to the present program. Such information as the amount of time spent by students in selected instructional areas, the number and percentage of students involved in selected programs, the use and distribution of professional time and talents, and the achievement records of selected student groups are all sources of valuable data. If these data were discussed with faculty groups, some assessment of the program would occur and more specific need areas would emerge.

Reality, as represented by such data, is difficult to ignore. The professional interested in instructional improvement must be prepared to cope with the typical human reaction to the kind of reality that suggests professional ineptness. Many staff members, including both teachers and administrators, will attempt to *project* problems ("It's the kind of students we have here . . ."), to *rationalize* problems ("Well, this is the logical result of the complex nature of education . . ."), or to *ignore* obvious conclusions ("So . . . ? That's what I expected . . .").

Inertia and tradition are two of the most powerful deterrents to significant change in education. In order to cause movement, it is first necessary to internalize a need to change—to motivate. After the data on present practices are analyzed, therefore, the next step is to match the data with the professional expectations, called "goals."

CLARIFICATION OF PURPOSE

While some might suggest that we have discussed educational goals and purposes *ad nauseam*, in order to begin a major change in an educational program it is vital to clarify and define our goals. Perhaps the lack of usability of goal statements in the past is related to the form in which the goals were stated.

If educational purposes could be stated in behavioral terms, a more definite picture of direction would be indicated. After goals have been stated in broad, general terms, then the more specific behavioral objectives that indicate goal achievement must be developed. These statements are much more specific, and communicate desired outcomes in observable or measurable terms. Much is now written in the literature concerning the use of behavioral objectives, and the interested reader is directed to one of these excellent references.[4]

The point is that, if our purposes could be clarified to the behavioral level, the evidence about present practice could be compared with our objectives, and the instructional strategies could be developed that would decrease any negative difference between the two factors.

If our present practice does not meet our expectations, then change is necessary. Let us assume that the change desired is in the practice and not in the expectancy. If this is true, then additional information is needed.

EXAMINATION OF NEW MODELS

At this point, those who will be involved in change need to be involved in the search for more effective procedures. Many sources of innovative practices are available through the Educational Research Information Centers (ERIC), several private foundations, professional journals and societies, as well as government agencies. As the search is mounted for viable alternates, those involved in the on-site visits to innovative schools should be cautioned against the "tire-kicking syndrome" that may afflict some educators. When visiting innovative programs, these individuals seem unable to grapple with the essential changes included, and seem unwilling to take ideas and procedures that might be applicable to their solution. Rather, they seem to examine negatively and superficially only the most obvious aspects, and take little with them. They seem to focus on why things *won't* work, as opposed to what *might* work.

Basic to this syndrome seems to be a lack of purpose, at least the lack of a purpose stated in behavioral terms. It becomes reasonable then that, if someone comes to visit an innovative program when they have no specific educational problem to solve, they might leave with no particular alternative that could be adapted to their situation.

If a set of behavioral objectives is clearly in mind to meet a clearly defined need, then *any* information source can be valuable. Once these sources are tapped and the decisions are made, related to the direction for implementation of change, reeducation and retraining become a necessary step that is too often overlooked by educational planners.

DEVELOPMENT OF NEW SKILLS

In order to decrease resistance to change, teachers and other staff members must be given the time and instruction to develop new and needed skills. Educational change agents too often bypass this vital step. The assumption seems to be made that, once a new educational model is identified, those

[4] See, for example, Robert Mager, *Preparing Instructional Objectives* (Palo Alto, Calif: Fearon Press), 1962, or Robert Gagne, *The Conditions of Learning* (San Francisco, Calif: Holt, Rinehart and Winston, Inc.), 1965, or W. James Popham, *The Teacher Empiricist* (Los Angeles, Calif: Aegeus Publishing Co.), 1965.

directly involved will adapt and, in fact, learn to implement it on their own. This generally does not occur.

The project at Hughson included money and time for the reeducation of those most directly responsible for making the changeover effective—the faculty. An initial summer workshop of six weeks gave these teachers the opportunity, not only to develop the skills of writing Learning Activity Packages, but also to examine and practice new teaching behavior required for the implementation of LAP system. A valuable adjunct was the greater staff cohesiveness that grew with the passing days. This phenomenon became functional as a protective device, the next "step" in planning for educational change.

PROTECTION OF CHANGE

Educational innovation is an extremely fragile phenomenon. The pressures from both community and professional sources to maintain the *status quo* are extremely strong. As any organization develops routines to implement policies, a constant danger is that these routines will become ends in themselves. Herbert Simon, as quoted by Miller, noted that routine drives out creative thinking.[5] A corollary to this statement might well be that routine-oriented people tend to drive out creatively oriented people. Therefore, those responsible for the operation of the educational organization itself need to plan a protection system for the people in the creative change process from both internal and external threats.

One source of internal threats to change comes from the bureaucratic process itself, where new ideas are beaten down with a club of forms and procedures. Many times it is necessary to revamp existing procedures with a special communication route, or a special "steering committee" of participating teachers or administrators, in order to increase the free flow of thought and ideas. An additional internal threat is the sense of isolation felt by a person doing something "different." Such individuals, whether administrators or teachers, require verbal and material support. The tendency to give up and return to past practices is somewhat similar to the smoker in the throes of "quitting again."

External threats to change emanate from the public as well as the professional community. Each school or district committed to a major innovation should authorize procedures to inform and extend the idea beyond the school walls. The Gallup Poll Organization reported statistics that showed that every segment of the school organization (board members, administrators, teachers, and parents) want planned change, but all feared the "general public" as a major deterrent to change.[6] This fear is warranted if the several publics are not informed of the purposes of the change and the major elements in the change itself.

[5] Miller, op. cit., p. 12.
[6] Gallup International, Inc., Princeton, N.J.

FEEDBACK FOR GROWTH

While the term "evaluation" suggests "good or bad," the term "feedback" is used here to imply the use of objective and subjective assessments that can be used as "channel lights" in the change process. If the objectives of the change have been defined in behavioral terms, then this step can be more effectively and efficiently accomplished because goal attainment is observable and measurable.

In addition, of course, is the necessity of program evaluation. The information collected can be used not only to evaluate hypothesized progress, however, but also to suggest ongoing alterations and adaptations to the program. A significant contribution of an innovation steering committee can be to collect and analyze pertinent data concerning the change and to suggest modifications in the program as the program is operating.

With the tremendous growth of innovation in education in recent years, the need to "tune up the staff" has appeared as an essential ingredient. The days of change through administrative directives have been swallowed up in the ground swell of teacher militancy and competency. We need new procedures for new times. The challenge is there, but without shared professional responsibility, in both the ends and the means of the process, we will find ourselves without educational progress.

IV

Organization

ONE OF THE interesting truisms that observers of educational administrative behavior have developed is that whenever two or more administrators get together, within half an hour they start describing their organization chart. The tenacity with which an educator will defend his organizational structure is frequently second only to the tenacity with which he will defend his family and loved ones. Nowhere else in the typical administrator's practices and policies does the pride of authorship influence his behavior to this extent.

The reason for the depth of feeling about organization is unclear. A few observations may help explain some of the behavior. It is rare to find an administrator who has an opportunity for his work to be as visible as his organization. Because of the visibility of his organization and consequently his vulnerability to criticism, he tends to be supersensitive about it.

Another reason for his sensitivity is that the chart describes the power structure of his organization and, as author of his organization, he has the authority to give and rescind power and prestige.

A major result of the concern about organization is that discussions of management behavior tend to begin and end with this topic. All too often discussions regarding the administration of schools have gone no farther than consideration of the organization. As mentioned earlier, organization is only one aspect of management, albeit an important management topic, and one that occupies a significant position in the manager's list of skills.

DEFINITION OF "ORGANIZATION"

One of the main reasons that organization is such a popular topic of conversation is that there are as many operational definitions of the term as there are practitioners. Perceptions of what is meant by "organization" vary from defining the supervisor–subordinate relationships to a description of the flow of resources. A common view is that the organization chart somehow represents the status of various functions, people, units, and positions within the organization. This tends to focus the consideration of the concepts underlying the various facets of organization on a series of lines and boxes. Too often judgments of considerable importance are made on the basis of a line diagram, not on what the diagram represents.

The fundamental precept of organization is simple. When a manager organizes, he divides up the work. The resulting grouping of people having responsibility for different tasks but sharing the same mission is called an organization. Whenever a task is divided or delegated, the organization has been changed. The organization is a constantly evolving entity; it is never static because the personnel, objectives, and environment are all constantly changing.

ORGANIZATION CHARTS

Organization charts are an attempt to represent reality on paper. Frequently the basic concept of organization begins and ends with the line drawing. Critics of organization charts criticize them because, they contend, organization charts tend to box people in and limit their freedom and prerogatives. It is important that the manager does not miss this elementary example of confusion between the means and ends of organization. The organization chart is a means toward dividing the work and toward communicating that division, not an end in itself.

An organization chart is also a representation of the resource distribution system. It is important that resources are broadly defined as money, personnel, and authority. Authority, in an organizational sense, is not only a superior–subordinate relationship but also the authority for decision making. An organization chart shows relationships between one organization group and another, and reflects how various functions, groups, and divisions within the organization relate to each other in the decision-making process. As with any chart, a chart depicting an organization tends to mirror reality; as such, it is never completely accurate and always distorts the image.

PRINCIPLES OF ORGANIZATION

One truth that seems to govern human behavior is that man can serve only one master. This truism is borne out in extensive management experience, but the importance of the concept is easily overlooked in day-to-day relationships within an organization. It becomes critically important, however, at times of stress. A staff member who has two or more superiors can be caught between differing viewpoints and confused about whose leadership he should follow. The typical result is that the staff member will tend to do nothing.

Clear lines of responsibility that provide only one superior for each subordinate will also prevent the possibility of a subordinate's being able to play one superior against the other. When one boss is put at cross purposes with another boss, the resulting confusion of leadership will compromise the effectiveness of the organization. A staff member who has only one superior has less probability of creating an empire within the organization than does one who has a potential of playing one superior against the other. A common argument against the one-man-one-boss concept is that it tends to decrease the creativity and possibilities of personal growth of the staff member. The same charge can be levied against an environment in which responsibility is undefined.

The key organizational element in any complex organization, such as a school system, is the unit president. Every manager must act as if he were the president of his own management team. In a typical school system this means the superintendent and those people who report directly to him. In a large school system this may also include a district superintendent and those principals and staff members who report directly to him. In an individual school the management team consists of the principal and the department chairpersons. The drawing on the next page shows this relationship in schematic form. Each triangle encloses a separate management team. The interlocking nature of the management teams provides that every person in the organization, with the exception of the superintendent and the department heads, is actually a member of two management teams. In other words, the assistant superintendent is a member of the superintendent's management team as well as the leader of his own management team consisting of the district superintendents of the areas for which he has responsibility.

Each management team should have its own plan for accomplishing its part of the overall mission. As the plans expand from the superintendent's office to the level of the individual teacher, they will become more precise, more student-oriented, and generally will involve a shorter lead time than those at the top of the organization chart.

A major benefit of careful attention to organizational concerns is that it helps define the roles of personnel involved in the organization. The definition of the parameters of activity will increase the efficiency and effectiveness of communication throughout the organization and should not be looked on as a constraint or a restriction of activities. Coordination among various levels and among functional groups will increase through improved understanding of the organization.

Another important reason for careful analysis of an organization is to clarify what decisions can be made by various functional positions. Most decisions are made on a consensus basis; when the organization is threatened, however, it is important for each member of the organization to know who has authority for making the necessary decisions. If this understanding is not widespread throughout the organization, con-

Interlocking Management Teams

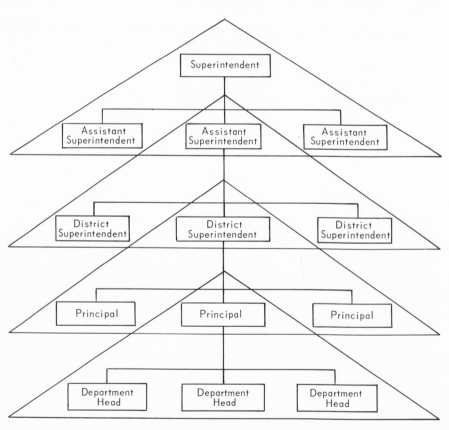

fusion results and the organization's effectiveness is seriously compromised.

One of the primary precepts in organization is that the entire management team assists in the planning activities of the particular organization. In the chart, the output of the assistant superintendents, combined with that of the superintendent, is the total output of the top management team. If any one member of the management team does not fulfill his or her obligation, the total effectiveness of the team will be diluted.

THE ORGANIZATION AND AUTHORITY

Another truism of organizational theory is that decisions should be made by the person lowest in the organizational hierarchy with the necessary information. This is the underlying concept of decentralization. Organizations will be effective only if the people making decisions have the necessary information and authority. As stated earlier, no amount of management or effective organizational practices will compensate for poor decisions.

In light of the heightened interest in decentralization over the past few years, it is important to keep in mind that the chief executive officer still retains total responsibility for the organization. He cannot give the responsibility away—he can only share it. The same is also true of any manager. The chief executive officer's role in regard to his authority is a different matter. Authority can be given away, subject, of course, to recall. The managers' ability to transfer the locus of responsibility, as compared to his ability to transfer locus of authority, is important to keep in mind as an organization develops.

The needs, abilities, and environment in which the organization finds itself are constantly evolving. To remain viable, an organization must remain dynamic and not become static. An organization chart should accurately describe how resources and responsibilities are actually distributed within the organization. For many reasons, some managers are hesitant to change their organizational structure. Although change for the sake of change is a poor criterion for determining the rate of evolution of an organization's structure, it should be kept in mind that the organization needs to be constantly undergoing change or at least careful scrutiny. If the formal organizational structure tends to remain constant, the organization often becomes a hindrance rather than a help in getting the job done.

When an organizational structure becomes a liability, personnel usually form new linkages, or alliances, that enable them to function. The resulting informal structure can dissipate resources and become counterproductive in achieving the mission of the organization. When there are differences between the formal and informal structure, the effective manager will minimize those differences. In ideal circumstances the informal and formal structures should be concurrent. The degree of discrepancy between the informal and formal organization indicates the degree of organizational ineffectiveness.

This discussion of organization has been limited in its scope to only a few principles. It is not intended to be an exhaustive treatment of the subject. As discussed in the opening paragraphs of this chapter, treatises on organization tend to be stylish and popular. Because of the interest in organizational style and fads, organizational ineffectiveness increases rather than declines. Too often the educational manager is tempted to modify his structure only to keep up with the latest style. Because organization is a way of dividing up the work, each organization is unique and should be treated individually. If the manager is serious in his quest to improve the effectiveness of his organization, the temptation to copy an organization chart from a reference book should be avoided at all costs.

The following articles are concerned with the organizational location of planning functions and do not address the topic of general organization. The location of the planner within the organization depends basically on the perception of his function and his relationship to the chief executive officer. The role definition seems to balance on the issue of whether the planner is a person who sees that the chief executive officer gets the necessary planning done, or the planner is a helpmate to the total organization. If he serves the chief executive officer, he is typically attached directly to his staff. If the planner serves the total organization, he usually is assigned further down the organizational hierarchy.

Merritt L. Kastens, "Who Does the Planning?" emphasizes the point that the planner does not plan but assists others in planning and that in many ways he is a teacher of planning.

A Society for the Advancement of Management special monograph by Edward C. Schleh points out that results should be the major consideration of organization theory as well as structure. The interrelatedness of the planning, organizing, and controlling functions of management is given extensive treatment.

The final article, by George S. Odiorne, summarizes this chapter by describing that the organizational structure must follow the objectives of the organization. Odiorne adds that any organization structure that will achieve those objectives is the appropriate organization.

Who Does the Planning?

MERRITT L. KASTENS

Planning Counselor
Hamilton, N.Y.

There is pretty good agreement on just what an ideal planner should be, particularly among the people who write the copy for the personnel-wanted ads in the *Wall Street Journal*. He should have a good solid grounding in finance and accounting as well as considerable experience in some aspects of the marketing function. If he is to work in a technically based company, he should have active experience in research or development. An engineering degree or an MBA—preferably both—is usually considered desirable. He should have some line experience in the industry with which he is involved but, in addition, should have a broad awareness of opportunities outside that industry. Increasingly, he is expected to have considerable skill in complex mathematical manipulations.

Furthermore, he is expected to have a fertile imagination, produce many new ideas, and have the courage of his convictions to present these ideas convincingly, orally and in writing. On the other hand, he is expected to be a master conciliator and arbitrator, to reconcile conflicting views into a mutually acceptable consensus without imposing arbitrary decisions in his own right. Finally, he is expected to have infinite patience and profound dedication, as a teacher and even evangelist, so that he can introduce his fellow managers to the value of a rational and orderly approach to their responsibilities.

This paragon should ideally be under 40 because if he is older than 40 he either (a) has too many fixed ideas, (b) is not sufficiently imaginative, or (c) costs too much money.

These specifications pretty much add up to the definition of an ideal president or at least an ideal general manager with the

Reprinted from *Managerial Planning*, January–February 1972.

addition of a somewhat godlike objectivity and a superhuman tolerance for frustration. It is therefore not surprising that the same management periodical that would publish the qualifications for this superplanner is very apt to have in the next article a strongly emphasized tract with the message: "The chief executive officer must be the chief planner."

There is obviously some confusion as to just what is a president and what is a planning officer. The confusion is undoubtedly grounded in ambiguities in the meaning of the words "plans" and "planning." This is not surprising in view of the great variety of meanings we all place on these words in both casual and technical discourse. However, if by "planning" you mean the setting of the long-term directions of the company, the deciding of priorities among objectives, and the relative allocation of resources, then this must be the senior executive's responsibility. Otherwise he is abdicating his position and not running the company.

The analysis of present situations, the structuring of alternatives, the sequencing of decisions, the coordination of the complex inputs, both factual and judgmental, available in an enterprise of any size are certainly valuable functions and normally would be the responsibility of a staff officer, whether he has "planning" in his title or not.

The attempt to differentiate these two kinds of functions is increasingly reflected in the appearance of titles like "coordinator of planning" or "director of plans" and similar modifications of the familiar "planning director" or "vice president of planning." This is all to the good. It is essential that there be this conscious differentiation of function if the power of formal planning to increase the validity of strategic decisions and accelerate corporate development is to be realized.

The most common cause of failure of the planning concept, and the source of much of the disillusionment that planning has engendered in many organizations, is the confusion betwen the decision-making or directing function and the analytical and structuring function.

The [problem] frequently arises because of a wishful hope on the part of the chief executive that some procedure, some "black box," or maybe some special breed of witch doctor can make his decisions for him or make his decisions automatic. If the president succumbs to this fallacy and the "planner" he hires is an aggressive sort, the planner may end up making the actual decisions from behind the throne and the CEO will find himself merely passing them on to the organization. The hazards of this Rasputin-type arrangement are quite obvious. The "planner" does not have the execution responsibility and has infinite avenues for evading the onus if the decision goes sour, whereas the man in the position of responsibility very seldom fully understands the rationale behind the decisions. The second phase of this situation is almost inevitable. The nature of the relationship cannot for long be hidden from the remainder of the executive structure of the organization and they may eventually mount a palace revolt, which will either remove the planning officer physically or isolate him organizationally in such a way as to eliminate his influence.

The alternative, and it is not so infrequent as you might think, is for the planner himself to end up as CEO. Such a move, of course, has the effect of recombining the decision-making authority with the responsibility. The prognosis in such a situation is not at all certain. In many instances it has worked out very well, in which case the so-called planner has merely taken a somewhat unconventional route to the top of the executive structure. However, very good planning technicians sometimes do not make good line executives or at least they have to undergo an additional learning period after they find themselves actually in the decision-making spot.

There is an alternative scenario for the president who decides to buy his company some planning "by the yard." He advertises for a planner, hires a well-qualified man, tells him to set up a planning department, and says: "OK, you make some plans for us." Then the president goes back to his office to go "to work." In this case the planning department produces a lot of reports, which are more or less widely distributed and sometimes read. The department, or at least the director, from time to time gets a pat on the head, perhaps through a mention in the annual report, and the next time there is a cost reduction program the planning department gets eliminated. The magic "black box" that the president bought didn't work, quite simply because it was never plugged into the circuit. The planner in this case is not really expected to make decisions. More critically, the decision makers are not committed to employ any planning-type thinking. So long as the management style of the company is not changed to provide for planned decision making by the responsible line executives, it is inevitable that the planning department will end up off in a back room somewhere, sometimes a rather lushly furnished back room, and ultimately fall victim to the valid criticism of being a bunch of ivory-towerites.

Incidentally, the planning professionals don't always resist this isolation as much as you might expect them to. It's rather fun to pursue the intellectual, analytical games of drawing up "credible scenarios" for the future of the company and then sort of sit back and say that if those dopes up in mahogany row were only smart enough to follow these schemes, what a terrific company this could be.

If we accept that the directing, decision-making, priority-setting aspects of planning can only be handled by the policy-making executives themselves, what does the "professional planner" contribute? Well, he is chief "whipper-in" to insure that the organization's planning cycle is completed on schedule. He coordinates and integrates substituent plans. He is coach and critic to the responsible executives in matters of format and structural logic. He and his staff make special studies and analyses and in general provide the quantitative planning inputs. Very often he is the unofficial arbitrator between conflicting points of view.

But actually he can take a still more active role in the planning process and still not usurp the essential decision-making role of his senior colleagues. A planning office can provide a procedural site to bring together various reactant ideas within the organization that might not otherwise have come into contact with one another and thus might have created problems. The "planner" can be the site where new ideas and new opportunities first react with the existing business system. To do this he must be in broad contact with the existing enterprise so that once he has absorbed and reacted to a new idea, he can bring about a secondary reaction with the appropriate unit of the existing structure, much as an active catalyst does in a chemical reaction.

Furthermore, he can so conduct his analytical activities that his numbers speak for themselves so loudly and clearly that strategic culs-de-sac are mercilessly exposed and developmental adventurism identified as the diversionary activity it often is.

But he can seldom do this except within a total management system that is attuned to rational processes and broad perspectives. If he deludes himself that he knows an incantation that will guarantee corporate growth and profits, he adds nothing to the intuitive, hunch-playing entrepreneur and invites his own eventual extrusion. If he tries to run the company from the back seat he is apt to demolish both planning and planner.

Given such a coherent environment, however, where the management recognizes the authority of well-organized facts and insists on rational structure in the consideration of strategic decisions, the skillful planning technician can make major contributions to the management process. He can maximize the probability of successful ventures and provide considerable protection against potentially catastrophic undertakings. He can facilite the concentration of resources in high-yield operations and save immense amounts of management time that might otherwise be dissipated in interminable meetings with ambiguous agendas. He can promote timely response to changing circumstances, and provide insurance against complacency. The one thing he is least likely to do is "plan" the future of the company.

The "Results" Approach to Organization

EDWARD C. SCHLEH

President, Schleh Associates
Palo Alto, Calif.

Ever since two men first worked together to accomplish a result, civilizations have been faced with organization problems. The decision as to who should do what, to what extent he should do it, and how one man's work should blend with the work of others has been a steadily increasing problem as civilizations have become more complex. The military structure seems to have been the first to recognize the advantages of principles and formal approaches in the problems of organization. Until fairly recently, however, little basic thinking seems to have been applied to the organization of enterprises other than the military. And what has been done seems mainly to have been copied from the military.

Efforts to define a "science of organization" have frequently tended to focus on definitions of formal structure divorced from the dynamics of people at work. These structures, in our opinion, have frequently been unrealistic because they do not recognize that people, not structures, accomplish things. There appears to have been an overconcentration on such devices as organization charts, organization descriptions, and the cataloging of positional duties and requirements. Too little consideration has been given to what we believe should be a fundamental objective of organization: *A job setup that encourages the most effective accomplishment from people toward the objectives of the enterprise, with proper weight given to cost, timing, resources, and general conditions that might prevent the accomplishment of these objectives.*

Reprinted from a special S.A.M. monograph.

DEFINE RESULTS EXPECTED

In an attempt to overcome the limitations in many conventional approaches to organization, we have developed what we call a "results" organization approach. This approach begins, of course, with the assumption that the total work to be done in an enterprise is simply too much for one man (A, Figure 1); therefore, he delegates. But, instead of saying he delegates "work"—things the man should do, or functions—we prefer to say he delegates responsibility for "results"; he asks other people to be responsible for the accomplishment of part of his results (B and C). The total of these parts, in turn, may be too much for a man; so he, similarly, asks others to take responsibility for accomplishing part of them (D and E, F and G). Thereby an overall organization plan develops.

You will note in this development a deviation from traditional organization structure. We do not talk about the general area of responsibility, or the requirements, or the work, but only about the *results* to be achieved. This, in our mind, is the starting point for real accomplishment by organization: concentrating on the objectives that will lead to concrete results. In effect, what you should ask is, "What are we trying to accomplish?" or, "What are we in business for?" These questions should lead to the results expected of the top jobs. As you go down the organizational line you should continue to ask, "What should this job accomplish that will further the overall objectives of the enterprise?"

Figure 1

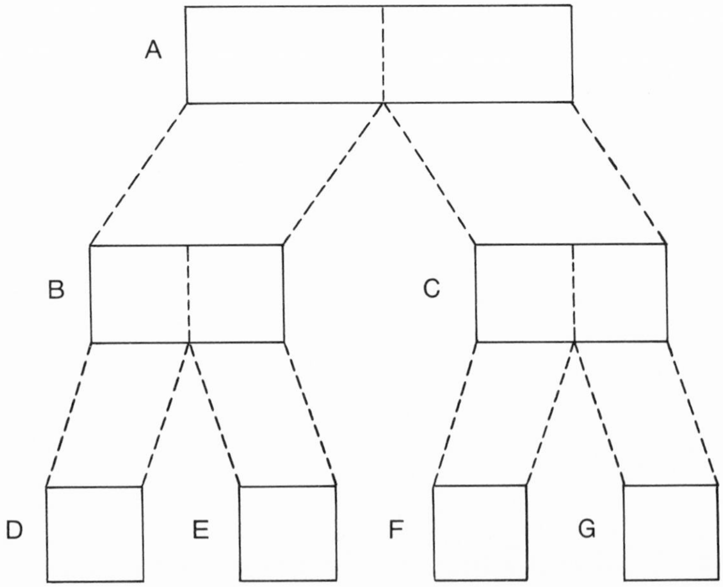

We should reaffirm that we are emphasizing *results*, not *activity*. Emphasis on activity is an error of many organizational systems: for example, responsibility for production of all company products, responsibility for sound salary administration and control, direct supervision of all salesmen in the northeast region. The vital questions arise: What is good "production"? What does "sound administration" mean? What should "direct supervision" accomplish?

Many management men feel that if you define responsibilities by function (which usually means by activity) you will automatically lead to a blended result. This viewpoint, in our opinion, is a fundamental error throughout much organization planning. People too often go in different directions unless you specify the results or objectives that you wish them to accomplish. The person in charge of a function too often yields to a human tendency: emphasis of certain phases of his function without regard to their proper relevancy to the overall objectives of the enterprise.

Many executives delegate responsibilities by the kinds of skills required. This, essentially, again is delegation by activity. It is defining jobs by similarity of activities rather than by similarity of expected results. It generally involves specialization; and while specialization is a basic principle in organization, it frequently has limitations. It often leads to a divided accountability for a result. Unfixed accountability is a forerunner of weak operation throughout an enterprise. The damage increases as an enterprise grows larger. More and more specialists come into the picture, all working toward the same result. Conflicts frequently develop. "No one" feels accountable for the final result. If the desired result finally is accomplished, it is often at an exorbitant cost.

Using the "results" approach to organization, you would try wherever possible to combine specialized activities whose end purposes are more or less identical. The exception to this principle would exist only in cases where tremendous gains are to be realized from specialization. In the setting up of staff functions the concept of specialization frequently hovers as a fetish and constitutes a rather widespread fallacy in organizational planning. In the misguided belief that a breakdown by specialty will lead to the most effective staff work, companies frequently have two, three, and sometimes four staff groups working toward the same objective from different points of view. For example, incentive engineers and personnel people may both be trying to achieve the same end result (more effective employee application to the work at hand); plant engineers and maintenance people may be aiming at the same basic objective (lowest machine cost per unit); certain public relations men and advertising men may be concentrating on the same final objective (increased sales). Personal conflicts and cross-procedures often arise among these specialists. Moreover, the arrangement usually confuses—sometimes antagonizes—line people wondering whom they should work with and who really is responsible. They are at a loss to decide which staff service should help them solve a particular problem.

At this point you might ask, "If we define jobs by results (and as specifically as possible), won't we be putting restrictions on the efforts of our people?"

Just the opposite is true! Definition by results places restriction on the "side"; that is, the extent to which a man may justifiably go in interfering with others. There is little restriction of his forward movements in achieving expected results. He is free to use his own abilities and ingenuity to achieve these results and to surpass them. This freedom leads to more effective utilization of personnel. Organization by *results* does not define the specific methods, approaches, or activities of the individual. Instead, it spells out the specific results the position should produce within the policy framework of the enterprise.

It is perfectly apparent that every man must know the results you expect of him if you want this kind of organization to be effective. These results should be in terms of specific objectives for a definite period. And especially important, *the person should be told, well in advance, explicitly what these objectives are!* Here, again, is a basic deviation from many organization descriptions. The duties and overall functions are often stated, but rarely get down to specific objectives for the individual man in terms of their blending into the overall objectives of the firm. Conversely, a "results" organization plan points naturally to specific objectives.

Lack of specific objectives leads to another (often ignored) organization problem. Many firms complain about their difficulty in getting their management people all the way down the line to feel a responsibility for improvement. In our opinion, organization planning itself has misled managements by implying that a responsibility for a function automatically assumes a responsibility for improvement. In practice this has not held true. Definition of jobs by "results," on the other hand, can and should be designed to include some improvement during each period. Since results should lead specifically to objectives for a particular period, improvement should be written in as a "way of life" for every period. The conventional description of duties, of general responsibilities, of things to be done routinely usually ignores the improvement factor. Consequently, such descriptions rarely stimulate each management man to make his contribution to the improvement of the operation on which he works.

Of course, the final accomplishments of an enterprise come from the combined work of a number of people. This suggests another requirement of good organization planning—that all results must blend together! You can readily see by Figure 1 that this blending is basic to a "results" approach, because every result delegated down the line is simply a part of the result expected above. Every person down the line has a responsibility to accomplish part of the overall results expected of the chief executive officer. This sense of mutuality throughout the enterprise encourages attitudes of cooperation. Each person in the enterprise has a "results" niche to fill.

There is a widespread feeling, unfortunately, that if a result is good, it is good without limit. (Witness the prevalence of open-end bonus plans.) We must remain alert to the fact that the principle of temperance applies to the stimulating of personnel just as it applies in every other area of human endeavor. In many instances a specific result desired by the enterprise may be achieved to a point beyond which it does little or no good. It tends then to gravitate toward a position where it begins to retard or harm the other operations of the enterprise. A typical case might be a plant quality problem. Beyond a certain standard that may be adequate to meet customer needs, tightening of quality may very quickly lead to excessive waste and high-cost operation. The same situation may exist in other areas. In sales, for example, there often is a limit to the value of such results as total sales valume, percent concentration, special product volume, and so on. There is a principle involved here. It might be described as the principle of "results optimity," and could be worded as follows: *For every desired result there is a limit or optimum level beyond which the operation may be damaged.*

The "results" approach to organization attempts to meet this problem by making men accountable for the negative as well as the positive results, in order to achieve and maintain balance. It has been stated as an organization principle that it is not wise to assign a man two responsibilities that are in opposition to each other. The results approach points up the fallacy of this proposition. In actual practice the best kind of organization, from a "results" point of view, develops a balancing of results so that the total-job objectives make each man hesitate to push any particular objective beyond the point where it is beneficial to the enterprise as a whole. Imbalance is best prevented, or cured, by accountability for positive and negative results. If a product development engineer, for example, can be held accountable for net profit realized in the first years of a product's life, he is automatically required to weigh such influencing factors as production costs, customer acceptance, and value of further refinements in the design.

Many firms believe it is more efficient to separate planning from doing, that there are certain top people best equipped for planning—perhaps staff people. To the contrary, one rule of the "results" approach is: *If a man has a responsibility for a result, tied into this is the responsibility to plan ahead in order to prevent any crisis that may keep him from accomplishing the desired result.*

A vice president should plan and propose all policies necessary to run his division or function most effectively. A foreman, in turn, should be expected to plan his crews and their work to meet efficiently all changing production needs. He should develop his own "grapevine" to provide needed information so that he can plan changes that are necessary to get the results expected of him. This combination of foresight and alert communications forces a decentralization of the responsibility for planning. It makes everybody a planner in the light of responsibility for assigned results. This responsibility for planning relieves the people at upper levels. It also forces a real accountability for the total job—something that the division of planning so frequently destroys.

GEAR STAFF TO ACCOMPLISHMENT

The "results" approach has a special application to staff services. Let us here define a staff man as "any man who must get a result through someone else who does not report to him or to his subordinates." As any enterprise grows there seems to be a natural tendency to add one staff function after another. This often occurs because specific problems arise that have to be solved. A staff service seems to be the obvious way to solve the problem. In other words, "Put a specialist on it." The "results" approach deals entirely differently with staff.

If there is one place where responsibility by activity is prevalent it is with staff functions. In typical organization structures these jobs often are defined with the responsibility for "advising," "consulting with," "assisting." All definitions of activity alone! Consequently, these staff functions usually are not accountable for specific contributions to the final objectives of the enterprise. Absence of accountability seems to follow from the rather popular thought that staff should be a service to the line but without any authority whatsoever. The implication exists that staff people should be happy to wait for the time when line may ask them for help, or else should constantly busy themselves with selling their activities. In our opinion, such a staff setup leads to fewer results from staff, a poorly blended result with line, and most frequently a body of frustrated staff specialists.

We have mentioned that staff also should be accountable for results. This accountability is in terms of the results achieved through its specialized medium of contribution to the total objectives of a job. It should harmonize with the efforts of the line people involved without reducing the latter's accountability for results.

Traditional organization philosophy has held that overlap in responsibilities is basically bad. From the point of view of the "results" approach, however, staff *always* overlaps with line. Should not both a methods engineer and a line supervisor be trying, in their respective ways, to achieve lower-cost methods of operating? Are not both the market research man and the sales force ultimately aiming for increased sales? This coincidence of final objectives is frequently misunderstood or overlooked.

It is important to recognize that overlap is a normal phenomenon and also that it can and should be exploited constructively and profitably.

In the belief that overlap between various staffs should be avoided, responsibilities have often been delegated by specialty. While there is no overlap in the specialized activity, there is actually repeated overlap between the staffs from the point of view of results. Since this has not been anticipated, it has almost invariably led to a dilution of responsibility on the part of the individual staff men concerned. It detracts from that sense of accountability so necessary to get a virile and driving organization.

Sometimes the staff problem takes on a different aspect. Let us compare long-range with short-range results for a moment. From the standpoint of type of knowledge required, both might well be combined. They have a similar knowledge requirement. However, from the point of view of getting results, long-range is very often inimical to the short-range. Compare capital engineering with current plant engineering; marketing trend analysis with territory studies; financial planning with cost control. Combining a responsibility for both short-range and long-range results in one job frequently leads to the sacrifice of one or the other or both. (Usually the short-range "hot" problems get the attention.) Wherever you can separate the long-range from the short-range, you frequently find that you get better results. This again is at odds with delegation by specialty. From that point of view there may be little reason for dividing up such activities. The results approach would separate them wherever possible. However, they must be defined so that short-range results are effectively blended into long-range results for sound operation.

If you are defining the results of staff, extreme care must be taken that these results are harmonious with the objectives of the line. Violation of this "results" rule can be a basic source of conflict between staff and line. The very definition of staff responsibilities by activity often fosters staff results that are *not* harmonious with those of the line. For example, a staff function may develop a fine report, a fine activity, a fine action, but these may not help the actual results the line is trying to achieve. Do cost records help a foreman find his own weak spots, or do they "show him up"? Does salary administration help stimulate men to more accomplishment, or merely "control" salary increases? Has a territory analysis resulted in more sales per salesman, or simply a new, unpopular division of accounts? If, however, you define staff functions so that they have a responsibility to get results, and these results are consistent with the line results—are part of the line results—you will find that there is a much greater inclination on the part of line and staff to work together. It is to their advantage!

If you have assured yourself of a real need for the staff function, if you have been very careful in setting up the results it is expected to achieve and the limits of its area of influence, if you have then made sure that these results are harmonious with those expected of the line, then staff should be given authority in form of the right of decision. The basic assumption is that staff people are specialists in their particular field and know more about it than the line people. We would, therefore, suggest the following principle: *In the particular, limited field in which staff operates, its decisions should hold unless proved wrong by the line.*

This, in essence, puts the burden of proof on the line. The suggestion runs counter to the practice of many firms. On the other hand, there is evidence that the principle has helped many staff people accomplish better results in their specialties. They do not then have to be supersalesmen. They can be hired for technical excellence with every expectation that their skill will be applied beneficially to the enterprise. Furthermore, they tend to be accepted by the line people because tangible results are expected of them and these results are harmonious with those expected of the line.

In order, however, to insure harmonious relationship between the two, it is essential that *both* staff and line get full credit for any accomplishments by the staff. A principle of dual recognition is involved here. This duality must hold even though one or the other appeared to do little in accomplishing the result. Any carping, any hesitation to share credit, any relieving of responsibility invariably will lead to friction between staff and line. Regarding staff particularly, it is most unrealistic to say that staff should be very happy in the knowledge that they have made a contribution and that perhaps "the word of the Lord" may someday descend upon them and give them recognition. All men want recognition, and as quickly as possible after it has been earned. Staff men are not exceptions. Any enterprise that fails to recognize this fact is simply unrealistic.

MAKE CONTROL LEAD TO ACTION

Let us look at the area of control, the record function. A common error of organization planning occurs in the accounting, financial, and other record functions. There is a popular assumption that these are top management control devices. Therefore, their basic function ostensibly is to notify top management of any errors that are occurring or have occurred. In our opinion, however, this type of functioning is calculated to lead to a strapping of actual operations, to poorer control, to less accomplishment, and to an excessive burden on the top management of the firm.

The "results" approach, on the other hand, incorporates constructive action into the record function. If your organization has set objectives for all management people down the line, the objectives can be tied into the records. On this basis, the following "action" principle becomes feasible for most record people: *A man charged with record keeping should not be responsible for record keeping or reports as such; he should be responsible for initiating action to correct deviations evidenced in the records.*

You will see, therefore, that the function of the record man would not be merely to develop fine reports for the purpose of "informing" top management. It would become his responsibility also to interpret his control instruments to all management people affected so that the latter can take appropriate corrective action.

This approach on control has four basic requirements if it is to achieve optimum effectiveness. First, a record must be current—current enough for line to take prompt corrective action. The typical accounting reports appearing two, three, and four weeks after the end of the month are just not current enough in many cases. Second, these records need not be extremely accurate. Remember, the purpose is to get action. In many cases, estimates will be just as effective as accurate statements. Third, these records must be *interpreted* by the record man so that only significant deviations are called to the attention of the person responsible for the results that are being measured. When a deviation is beyond the basic authority of that person, it should be reported to the person above him—but only at that point. Fourth, the interpretation should be made in the first instance *to the man,* not to his boss. The man himself is given first chance to correct the problem. This approach is at variance with typical control procedure.

Under the "results" approach a record function becomes a valuable tool to each management person reported on. The record man is a friend, a helper, an aid in achieving the results that each man is expected to achieve. He is on the team. He is not the supersleuth who eagerly pounces on any possible error in order to proclaim it proudly to top management.

REFLECT EXPECTED RESULTS
IN AUTHORITY AND ACCOUNTABILITY

How does the "results" approach view authority? In many firms, there is a feeling that if you *state* to a man that he has full authority, this means he *has* full authority. Nothing could be further from the truth. A man has full authority only if he *feels* that he has it.

In the "results" approach we would look at authority simply from one point of view: the errors expected to get a result. In general, authority would be "the right to make errors." To the man on the job, this usually is the real meaning of the right of decision and command.

The executive or supervisor should define the results he expects of a man on a job. He should then ask himself this question: "If I, or anyone else, were to go after these results, what kinds of decisions would I be required to make?" He should further ask himself: "If I were to make those decisions, what would be the typical errors I might make?" He should then tell the man on the job that he may make these kinds of errors (and the total number of them) during a specified period with impunity—and we stress *impunity*. At the end of a period, however—perhaps six months or a year—the man must be accountable (and so understand from the outset) for the overall accomplishment of the results expected, the sum total of the errors he has made, and their cost. This approach leads to a widening horizon of authority. Men are more willing to "stick their necks out," to use initiative, to be creative. They develop better because this approach recognizes the fundamental rule that all men learn by doing, and are not immune to mistakes during this process.

Of course, any definition of results or authority is meaningless unless it leads to a final accountability for results. Each man must feel that he will receive equitable credit or blame, depending on whether or not he accomplishes the results expected of him. This personal assurance is essential in any "results" approach. On the opposite side of the picture, you might do well to consider objectively the effects of personal accountability of such activities as appraisal plans, promotion plans, employee relations methods, and pay systems. Pay plans based on seniority, year-end uniform salary increases, blanket "merit" increases—in general, pay increases not based on specific results you expect of the job—all tend to weaken personal accountability for results. On the other hand, a compensation plan closely tied to desired results acts as an effective stimulant in getting men to strive toward agreed-on objectives.

The same tends to be true for appraisal and promotion systems that are not closely tied in with specific results expected from the jobs: a weakening of personal accountability. Some appraisal systems in vogue the last several years are based primarily on individual traits, on duties, or on personality factors, with comparatively little weight given the specific results that should be expected of the position. This evil sometimes is aggravated by the use of group appraisals, thereby further relieving a direct supervisor of accountability for results delegated by him to his subordinates. It is only by strengthening the supervisor–subordinate relationship, through a real accountability for results, that sound accountability can be obtained. Appraisals should be designed to encourage this relationship and this accountability.

Another factor affecting accountability is the mode of committee operation. (In this treatise we would consider any group of two or more people a committee, whether it meets formally or not.) In recent years, with the emphasis on group dynamics, it appears to us that there has been an inordinate stress on group action as the best way to get desired results. Consequently, there is evidence that more and more organization structures are favoring committee action, and group action generally, as the means of getting desired action. The "results" approach takes a rather dim view of this. Too frequently, such committees or groups tend to relieve men of accountability for the results assigned to them. These group arrangements often permit an individual to bring his personal problems to one or more other people for review and consideration. Then, if something goes wrong in his area of responsibility as a result of a decision backed up by the group, he feels he is somewhat relieved of personal accountability for results. There usually follows a flood of explanatory reports to "everyone." As a rule of thumb we suggest that whenever you find there are many reports circulating to "inform," there usually is at the root of these reports a lessening of personal accountability for expected results.

Tied into accountability is the problem of balance. Many people feel that concentrating on one problem at a time is better than diversification of effort. The feeling generally is expressed in some such statement as, "It is better to shoot with a rifle than a shotgun." Inordinate attachment to this sentiment leads many companies to an imbalance of achievement. We suggest it is better, as a general rule, to achieve some accomplishment in each of the results expected of a position, or throughout an enterprise, than to concentrate on only one or two. (We recognize, of course, that some objectives must be viewed from a longer time perspective than others.) A typical overall example of imbalance is the excessive concentration in one year on cost reduction, only to be followed in the succeeding year by a 20 percent drop in sales, because of failure to plan a hard-hitting sales program, and consequent loss of all the gains made through the cost-reduction program. The imbalance in such instances can, of course, occur in the reverse way; excessive concentration on meeting customer schedules may gradually dilute feelings of accountability to produce at minimum cost.

Imbalance sometimes occurs in a more directly human way. A supervisor may have five or six people working under him. Two or three may be inept, one may be very capable. When a difficult problem arises in the results expected of one of the weak members, the supervisor's natural inclination is to ask the strong man to shoulder and solve the difficulty. In this way, more and more the strong man finds troublesome problems steered his way.

In due time he probably finds his own expected job results difficult to achieve. Under the circumstances, and without too much twinge of conscience, he may let some of his own job obligations go by the board. Before very long he begins to feel less and less accountable for the results of his own job.

Notice, on the other hand, what happens to the weaker employees in situations of this kind. They become even weaker! They have been relieved of accountability for the overall results they are supposed to achieve, for someone else is handling their difficult problems for them. This is a dilution of accountability for results. It is a common circumstance where organization planners follow a principle (one we believe to be fallacious) that says, essentially, that organization structure should be designed around the person. All too often this design simply leads to lack of accountability for results throughout the enterprise; consequently, to a weakening of effective organization. It tends, actually, to perpetuate weaknesses instead of preventing or eliminating them.

CONCLUSION

As you carry through on the "results" approach to organization you are, in effect, trying to develop each job down the line as a small replica of the job above. It is commonly stated that jobs at the top are entirely different from those down below. This thinking usually leads to a rigid and costly organization structure. There should be judgment at all levels, judgment in relation to the results expected. Men should be expected to develop ingenuity and sound judgment at every level, and act as responsible management men in carrying out the specific results they are expected to achieve. Each job, on this basis, should have the broadest scope possible for accomplishment of the results expected. This intelligent latitude is a most effective way to develop people for promotion within the organization because they are at all times learning to do the kind of thinking expected in the job above, only in a more restricted sphere of operations. This self-growth at every level also has the effect of relieving upper management of the excessive detail of doing all the thinking down the line, thinking based very frequently on inadequate facts.

Overall, the "results" approach to management organization tends to develop to the full the innate abilities and talent of every person in the organization. It contrives to get them behind sound objectives. It allocates to each of them his share, his personal share, of the responsibility for accomplishment. It attempts to reverse the insidious trend that has developed in the past several years, that of assuming that working at something is getting something done.

New forms of corporate organization are coming into their own as many executives decide the pyramid is "square"

Up the Pyramid . . . er . . . Doughnut . . . er . . . Beehive!

GEORGE S. ODIORNE

Dean, School of Business
University of Utah
Salt Lake City, Utah

Doughnuts, grapes, and beehives.

Those aren't items on a grocery list. They're descriptions of some of the new forms of corporate organization gaining favor in the rapidly changing seventies.

"Take five separate product divisions, then try to sell three of the five products to one market segment—say utilities. When you do that, conventional organization charting isn't worth a cent." Thus states the president of a large multiproduct firm.

Or take the case of a giant retailing firm.

"When we had one large downtown department store," an executive says, "we had a conventional organization chart. Now we have branches as well as the big store—plus a lot of supplier firms, and a few wild-shot operations spread around. How could you make that fit the old chart?"

These are two of the simpler kinds of problems faced by corporations today. The problems have led to a quite revolution in corporate organization.

Result: A variety of organization forms never imagined by the experts who produced the once-hallowed and now all-but-outmoded organization chart that resembled the pyramid.

Reprinted from *Nation's Business*, January 1972.

UNDER FIRE

Everybody, it seems, is taking potshots at the old-fashioned pyramidal style.

Ex-Avis chief Bob Townsend, in his semihumorous book, *Up the Organization,* suggests that you can do best by chucking your organization chart altogether. It "strangles profit and stifles people," he says.

Canadian savant Lawrence Peter argues that managers tend to rise in an organization to their level of incompetence and then stay there. He suggests that the organization chart is partly at fault.

Now, instead of the massive pyramid, we have a stretchable rubber sheet.

What are the major trends in this flexible approach to corporate organization?

Some of the latest models have names like matrix, bottom-up, collegial, ladder, beehive, project management, task force, or doughnut.

Confronted with such an array, how does an executive distinguish between them? More important, how does he decide whether any is useful in shaping his own organization?

A close look shows that organizational forms tend to fall into two categories.

One starts with the assumption that all authority and responsibility ultimately rest at the top of the organization, except for those things specifically delegated to lower levels. This is a traditional kind of organization, which is ruled by procedures and directives and has a chart showing who are the order givers and who are the order takers.

The other starts with the assumption that the authority of people in an organization to act is unlimited except where there is a specific policy or law that prohibits such an act. It also assumes that the objectives are clear, and it's often associated with firms where management by objectives is the operating system. This is an energy-releasing kind of organization, where anybody who has a good idea related to his objective goes ahead and carries it out—if it hasn't been explicitly forbidden.

The second approach seems to be that behind most of the new organizational forms.

Let's look briefly at some of the major varieties.

Bottom-up management. Originated by William Given, former president of American Brake Shoe (now Abex), this is designed to push the decision-making power and initiative down to the lowest possible level in the organization.

Stronger delegation, more responsibility at lower levels, and plenty of authority to act are its essential features. It has been rather widely adopted in various ways by many American corporations.

Collegial management. More widely used in Europe than America, this deals with the very top levels of the firm.

The name means that the organization pyramid doesn't have a single head but a group in charge. This is sometimes called "the office of the president" or perhaps "executive committee," and is occupied by two or more executives of equal status.

The beehive. The final chart here resembles the outline of a beehive.

The system is three-dimensional and consists of a series of concentric rings on top of one another. The people at the vice presidential level, for example, constitute one ring, the plant managers another.

The boss in that circle becomes sort of a queen bee. The chart attempts to show relationships at human as well as formal levels. The result is better personal relations, improved communications.

Project management. The organization looks something like a bunch of grapes hung under the organization chart. When one ripens and falls off (i.e., the project is completed) the people go back to their regular organization chart boxes until a new project comes along.

This has grown to be the dominant form of organization in both government-sponsored and private corporate research.

Says one pharmaceutical research chief: "We found that research budgets went up and new products went down year after year, until we threw out the departmental format for doing research. Now, we only use our departments of chemistry, virology, microbiology, computer science, and the like as home departments out of which we pull people for the projects, named after the objective we want to accomplish, such as a measles vaccine or some similar product."

The doughnut. Resembles the beehive, but is really a two-dimensional chart of concentric circles.

The top officers constitute the inner ring, with staff specialists in such areas as personnel, finance, legal, and engineering work in the second ring, not reporting to any particular officer, but accessible to all.

The third ring consists of divisional general managers or subsidiary company presidents, not responsible to any single officer as they would be in a divisionalized organization with general managers reporting to group vice presidents.

C.I.T. Financial Corp. has done well operating under this kind of circular chart. President Walter Holmes says the organization has achieved a "high degree of rapport" among managers at every level.

Some see this as the right format for conglomerates, whose units are so diverse that no other clustering of groups seems to fit.

The matrix. If a company has a variety of products with a sales force for each, it may run into trouble when it takes a whole package to a new market. For example, Honeywell makes temperature-control devices, switches, computers, valves, and cameras. How can the company sell them to a big market, like public utilities? It might, for example, have salesmen from each division tramp into the purchasing managers' offices, but this would be costly and perhaps ineffective.

One solution is to create a product management position with responsibility for putting together packages of Honeywell products suitable to utilities, and selling them the package. This lateral slice across autonomous divisions, all of them aimed at special markets, is the essence of the matrix form of organization.

Professor John F. Mee of Indiana University, a major architect of the matrix system, suggests it will be a dominant form of organization as we get more complex products and more sophisticated managers.

The test for most companies is the profit yield, which appears to be high as new markets and applications for existing lines emerge. The system also produces ideas for whole new lines to research, and for engineering developments.

The ladder. Similar in design to the matrix, this is an attempt to get more output in large companies from growing numbers of staff experts. In a conventional organization chart you have a layer of them just below the chief executive. Here, you slip them out and stretch them vertically—like a ladder—along the side of the chart. Thus they resemble the gantry crane used to service a huge missile.

The experts can enter the organization at any level and have quick access to the spot where they are needed most. That way they avoid being tied up by protocol before they go into a situation to help.

The ladder can also be used for special career patterns and routes to higher pay for scientists. Take Dr. X, who is a great scientist but somewhat less than talented in administration. Ordinarily, unless he is promoted to a vice presidency, he couldn't expect to make it big financially. But all vice presidents in the corporation have administrative duties.

The answer?

Parallel ladder routes to the top.

Because Dr. X is an inventor and a genius in technical matters, he can get raises on the technical ladder that equal those of a line vice presidency, yet the company isn't obliged to inflict his disruptive leadership on the rest of the organization.

In one national electronics research firm, the main inventor is a vice president, but a close look shows that he is in charge of only one person—himself.

The task force. This is an old plan that has taken on new vitality since the traditional organization chart has been losing favor. The task force should be centered on a specific objective, with time and budget commitments clearly stated. One of its main advantages is that it lends vitality to a job.

The old bureaucracy is replaced with what one wag has called an adhocracy, referring to the task force's temporary nature.

Unlike some government commissions that, once established, are never disbanded, the task force folds up when its job is done.

This has lots of advantages. You can get people to serve on a task force who would balk at a standing committee. They know that when the goal is reached, the team disbands.

OUT WITH THE OLD?

Do all these innovations mean that the ordinary forms of organization planning and charting are obsolete? Do we no longer have line and staff, with divisions, functions, and departments?

Obviously, we won't throw them out completely. Many leading corporations, including General Motors, Ford, General Electric, IBM, and Du Pont, still operate in this manner.

The reason for doing so, however, is not to conform to some theoretical "law of organization." Rather, it's to use a form of organization that will get the company where it's going faster than any other form will.

The big change is not in organization charts but in attitude. Managers are paying more attention to company and unit objectives. Once you know where you want to go, organization charts and planning become means for getting there.

Thus the best advice for executives is: Get your objectives clear and organize in the way that is most likely to help you achieve them. If, in the process, you have to throw out some old organizational theories, don't worry. If they won't work, they weren't very good to begin with.

V

Control

CONTROL INSURES THAT management's plan is achieved. The concept of control is broad, encompassing many types of activities that enable the organization to achieve its mission. If planning is the keystone of educational management, control must be the capstone. Without adequate control procedures, the probable success of a plan is almost nil. As one of the most important responsibilities of the manager, control needs continuous attention.

The concept of control that has been accepted by the management profession includes all those activities that a manager does to insure that the plan of the organization is accomplished. Depending on the sophistication of the organization and the complexity of its activities, control procedures may include nothing more than the principal's glancing up from his desk to see that there are no children left standing after the school buses have departed at the end of the school day. This simple control procedure may be contrasted with the more elaborate mechanism to insure that the provisions of a performance contract are being fulfilled by the contractor.

The field of finance provides an analogy that frequently helps clarify the control concept. A budget helps insure that the intent of the organization is carried out through the expenditure of available funds. It is a means of indicating when deviations from the plan occur and signaling that corrective action needs to be taken.

DEFINITION OF CONTROL

Control procedures establish the limits or boundaries of acceptable activities in which a person or organization may take part. The boundaries enable the individual manager to exercise all the freedom available to him within the area prescribed by the boundaries. Because the boundaries have been drawn, the manager has been provided with more freedom than he would have without them. When no boundaries exist, behavior tends to be inhibited because of the constant fear of disapproval. It is well known that people respond favorably to success and positive reinforcement. This understanding is the basis of most control procedures and mechanisms. When the difference between acceptable behavior and unacceptable behavior is not clearly understood by all parties concerned, the resulting behavior is constrained. Conversely, when the difference between acceptable performance and unacceptable performance is known, the probability of acceptable behavior is increased.

TYPES OF CONTROL

There are as many types of controls as there are organizations and types of activities conducted by those organizations. As mentioned at the beginning of this chapter, the budget has historically been a useful type of control. It has tended, however, to give the major decision-making responsibility to the person with custodial responsibility for the budget. It demonstrates a form of control that has historically been used in school systems in the type of exception reporting described in the following example.

So long as a teacher does not exhibit behavior grossly deviant from the norms of the social milieu of the community, he need not fear dismissal. The tight restrictions on the social and personal behavior of educational personnel of half a century ago that typically involved smoking, drinking, dating, and church attendance are examples of constrictive kinds of controls.

A more positive concept of control for education personnel is demonstrated by the following example.

As long as a teacher is able to produce a certain amount of learning for each member of his class, he has freedom to do whatever he would like within the legal behavior constraints that are part of his job description.

A similar statement could be made describing the work of the principal. He can utilize his resources in any manner he desires as long as certain prescribed learning outcomes are achieved by an appropriate number of students.

An important point in the use of control techniques in the previous paragraph is that outcomes or objectives and strategies for achieving them are controlled, not people. The difference between the possibility of a big-brother type of manipulation and the concept of control described in the previous paragraph is significant. The constraints on the behavior of people are considerably fewer when control is viewed in the manner described. In fact, freedom of the individual has increased, as an intellectual concept and in actual behavior, by focusing on plans and not on people. Improved morale and fewer personal conflicts within the organization are almost certain if adequate control procedures are used. Likewise, if people never know when they are subject to reprimand, serious morale problems can result.

A moment of reflection will reveal that an event can be monitored, changed, modified, or stopped either before the event has occurred or while it is occurring. Thus control procedures can be defined as pre-operational or operational.

PRE-OPERATIONAL CONTROL

Pre-operational control procedures provide automatic responses whenever the barriers of acceptable performance are threatened. An example of a pre-operational control is that if more than 15 percent of the student body of a particular school are infected with a contagious disease the school is closed. Another example is that if more than 10 percent of a class do not achieve at least 80 percent of the expected achievement level on a reading test, a detailed evaluation of the reading program will be conducted.

OPERATIONAL CONTROL

Operational controls are historically commoner in educational settings than are pre-operational controls. A classical example of an operational control is the removal of a child from a classroom when his behavior becomes too disruptive. Another example of an operational control is the keeping of a child in from recess for not adequately preparing for his spelling test. In modern management activities, operational controls are used as sparingly as possible, and only in cases when viability of the organization or individuals within the organization is seriously jeopardized should they be used. The teacher, principal, and all other managers should be allowed freedom to pursue their own methods except in those few cases when the integrity of the organization is in danger or personal or professional harm may be done to individuals.

THE CONCEPT OF CONTROL: A NEGATIVE IMAGE

The concept of control is probably the most misunderstood and castigated concept of management. The concept suffers from having a name that invokes negative images in the minds of many people. These negative thoughts are accentuated in a profession such as education with a long-standing tradition of freedom. The unfortunate image of control seems out of place with the concept of academic freedom in the community of education.

Many writers have attempted to resolve the problem of the negative image of the concept of control by simply ignoring the concept and not using the word. Many writers have alluded to the ideas of control by describing a type of preventive maintenance for organizational problems. They have described various techniques for indicating when attention is demanded, but few have attempted to mold these techniques into one broad concept.

It is tempting to suggest that a new word is needed for the concept of control. Aside from the questionable attempt at deception by substituting a new name for an old concept, one must be less than enthusiastic about the chances for success of such an adventure. A more prudent strategy seems to be to educate large numbers of educational managers in the nuances of the concept of control and thereby eliminate the emotional reaction to the word.

One of the factors that has contributed to the confusion and misunderstanding of the control concept is the abuses that have occurred in management. The word seems to conjure up highly regimented workers in an assembly line type of organization. Although this type of abuse has occurred and still does occur, it is unfortunate that the concept should be held accountable for the abuses. The rational fear of the big-brother type of supervision is an important part of the American culture.

As with any management tool the concept of control is amoral in that it has the potential for abuse as well as the potential for positive use. By better understanding the concept, the manager increases the prospects for constructive use and decreases the prospects for distructive application. The more widely known and understood the concept becomes the more efficient and effective our educational systems will become.

The article that follows describes the various levels of controls within an organization. The author uses examples from the National Aeronautics and Space Agency that, in many ways, are directly transferable to the educational enterprise. In the opening section of this book an article, "The Principles of Management," devoted several pages to the concept of control.

These two articles illustrate control procedures from both an operational and a theoretical point of view. The reader is urged to study how the theory has been applied in the reality of the space program.

The Many Dimensions of Control

LEONARD SAYLES

Professor
Graduate School of Business
Columbia University
New York, N.Y.

The subject of management controls is one of the oldest in the field of administration. No matter which theory or system of management one favors or practices, controls inevitably turn up as a central element—and properly so. After all, controls are the techniques by which the manager decides to expand his most valuable asset, his time. Be they formal or informal, it is through controls that he knows where things are going badly that require his intervention— and where and when he can relax because things are going well. All managers from presidents to foremen make use of controls, some more effectively than others.

We have recently finished a review of the management of the National Aeronautics and Space Agency, extending from first-line technical managers and project managers up to the top of the agency. Although NASA has many special complications that wouldn't be found in most companies, its experience in the use of controls has direct relevance to any organization, public or private. Therefore, what follows is a general discussion of the use of management controls, with examples drawn from the space program.

Perhaps more problems are created by the manager's failure to recognize differences among types of control than by anything else. As we begin to look more closely at the functioning of any large organization, we observe four quite distinct types of control that perform very different functions for the manager.

Reprinted from *Organizational Dynamics,* Summer 1972.

1. *Reassurance to sponsors.* Higher management and sources of funds and support need reassurance that the major objectives are likely to be met efficiently and on time.

2. *"Closing the loop."* The manager seeks to prove that technical and legal requirements have been met, and therefore that neither he nor the program is vulnerable to obvious omissions.

3. *Guidance to subordinates from managers.* The subjects their superiors pay attention to, as demonstrated by both written documents and informal observations, give guidance to subordinates as to what is important and what they should concentrate on.

4. *Guidance to lower-level managers by higher management.* Perhaps the most important function of controls is to direct the attention and energies of managers to subjects and locations where accomplishment is lagging and management action is required.

We shall term number 1 high-level controls, number 2 low-level controls, and numbers 3 and 4 middle-level controls, the last being both the most important and the most easily neglected.

HIGH-LEVEL CONTROLS

In a large organization, top management needs to be convinced that any individual program is reasonably efficient in moving toward its major goals. At the simplest level, this might mean showing the percentage of the total program completed in a given fiscal year. If possible, it is always useful to show that either the rate of completion or the rate of accomplishment per dollar of expenditure is improving.

The distinctive feature of these high-level measures is that they are intended to reassure those who are not sufficiently close to the scene to be able to see any of the detailed activities or to evaluate them. If properly done, they may ward off investigatory activities and provide sponsors and top management with ammunition to counter skeptics and the opposition. These measures, therefore, have a public relations quality about them, and it is unfortunate that a good deal of internal effort may have to be expended to accumulate statistical information to support preestablished contentions. Nevertheless, in any large organization, public or private, the higher echelons are sufficiently far removed so that they require this type of reassurance.

The business enterprise has the advantage of a slightly less arbitrary system called profit accounting, but its limitations in measuring managerial performance are also well known. Changes in inventory evaluation, decisions as to which costs will be capitalized and which will be expensed, formulas for "distributing" overhead, and similar accounting decisions can influence profitability by a modest factor of 100 percent or more. Even the general public is beginning to realize that profits are rather arbitrary numbers that can be manipulated within a wide range.

High-level controls are not controls in the usual management sense of the term. However, in complex endeavors necessitating substantial expenditures to complete high-risk programs that require many years to show results, it is necessary to provide some regularized feedback to those whose dollars or reputations are involved. The measures that are used demonstrate but do not prove efficiency, nor do they provide adequate bases for continuing supervision.

By this we mean simply that these reports demonstrate that managers are trying to improve performance, but they are not adequate measures of real performance. We are reminded, by analogy, of consulting firms installing new incentive plans that cut labor costs by 25 percent or even 40 percent. The reports made to top management appear to more than justify the investment in heavy installation costs. What the reports don't disclose is the increasing number of grievances over standards and the time and money involved in their settlement, the growing foreman–worker antipathy over the incentive program, and the costs of the continuing industrial engineering needed to update standards as jobs and technology change, as well as the growing resistance to technological change caused by the constant need to negotiate new standards. Added together, as they rarely are, these may show quite a different "profit" on the new incentive plan!

LOW-LEVEL CONTROLS

Low-level controls are checking procedures established to insure that neither financial nor technical decisions are taken without adequate review, and that no necessary step has been omitted. Such procedures as these are typical examples:

- All expenditures over $500 have to be approved by the controller's office.
- When "off standard" temperature prevails for more than five minutes, written authorization from the chief engineer is required to continue processing procedures.
- Storage of flammables within 50 feet of Building 209 requires the permission of the safety officer.
- Any substitution of materials must be approved by the subsystem engineer, the functional manager, and a representative of the project office.

These are old hat in classical scientific management, but they present recurring problems. Perhaps the most obvious problem is the predecision as distinct from a postdecision position of these controls. Nervous managers want to know before, of course, but every advance check is a potential delay; when there are many such checks, gaining the required authorizations, permissions, and what have you can hold up work on a specific problem for weeks or even months.

Important decisions are often subject to before-the-fact review by a number of people. Thus, in a technical program, a design decision by an engineer may be reviewed by his functional manager, a technical specialist in the project office, the project manager, and then the program office. In addition, parallel system managers may also be involved. Such "sign offs" are time-consuming both for the project and for those who must review the technical details. When there are a great number of these to be made, there is a temptation for each echelon to give just a cursory glance.

Many after-the-fact checks are done on a sampling basis to assure functional managers that adequate technical expertise is being utilized and existing organizational policies are being upheld.

One of the most serious defects of these low-level controls is that they divert energy from critical problems to those where someone is checking up. It is the "numbers game" with which every experienced manager is familiar. Efforts are diverted to making oneself and one's department look good at the expense of larger goals and often at the expense of other managers.

The manager of the "frame and mechanics" unit, for example, was approached by the manager responsible for final assembly, who asked whether he would put some re-engineering efforts into reducing frame weight. It was clear that weight was an increasing problem and the total system would not get through final acceptance tests at the rate that the weight was increasing. The frame manager nodded agreement, but he knew he would do nothing. In the history of these projects, he knew that weight was always a problem, and furthermore one to which many managers contributed. The problem wouldn't get critical until the final tests, at which point it would be a problem for everyone, meaning no one—he wouldn't be blamed. On the other hand, if he diverted engineering effort now, a subsystem test next week might be in trouble, and those test results were watched closely by his boss. This manager minimized his potential losses by ensuring that a problem that involved him personally wouldn't occur next week and risking minor trouble a few months from now when the overweight problem would come up.

Many observers have noted what game theorists have called the "minimax" solution to individual efforts to cope with win–lose situations. The manager consistently chooses a decision by which he is guaranteed to minimize his losses, rather than seeking a large payoff at the risk of a big loss.

One all-too-common expression of the playing-it-safe syndrome is making sure that all rules, procedures, and orders are followed and that easily measured quantitative bench marks are met. Then, if a problem emerges, it can be argued that it is the "other guy's fault" because everything specified was done, as proved by the check results. Naturally, this hinders responsiveness to larger system interests, to facilitating the work of groups who may need your collaboration or modifications in your procedures, and who are dependent on your being flexible. The controls introduce rigidities that can become a serious problem whenever the work is not routine, the technology has intrinsic uncertainties, and the employee is not simply doing the same thing over and over again repeatedly.

Evidence of management concern in most organizations over these control-induced rigidities shows itself in the extent to which middle and upper management seek to see what is really happening, as distinct from what the controls tell them. Even relatively high-level managers, particularly when dealing with advanced technologies, seek to gain a feel for the raw technical data. They are not content to look at staff summary or exception reports. Nor is their concern misplaced. Evidence suggests that this immersion in technical detail is necessary to keep abreast and knowledgeable. Some even insist on sampling all the original correspondence concerning project progress and problems. Of course, this raises the obvious question of whether technically unsophisticated managers can properly serve in these posts.

Typical of this point of view is the following remark made by a project office engineer:

> There is just no substitute for having the technical sophistication and willingness to go into the other guy's shop and look around. In R&D you've got to find out what he is not willing to tell you. The estimates, the test reports, and the progress reports tend to be too optimistic, and you'll go under every time if you take them at face value. The designers are always optimistic about future performance, and the project people naturally cover up their problems, so you've got to be their technical equal and get into the real data to know where you stand.

Of course, this effort also represents what we have called middle-level controls—that is, assessing the organizational effectiveness of various contributors to the system and seeking to predict where breakdowns are likely to occur.

MIDDLE-LEVEL CONTROLS

Middle-level controls are signals that guide managers to act in ways that contribute to overall systems effectiveness, not to paper "wins" or immediate payoffs. They concentrate on what is necessary to keep the organization functioning. As techniques for keeping in touch with the progress of the dispersed parts of the program, assessing information received, and responding to a variety of information inputs, they are vital to any project manager. The project manager here is no different from any manager; handling middle-level controls is the heart of his job because it determines where and when he must go into action.

Much of traditional management literature dealing with delegation and controls stresses the autonomy that must be given to subordinates for motivational reasons. The superior waits to intervene until the subordinate has manifestly failed; otherwise he stays out of the process.

This is a luxury that the manager and the organization can't afford. In the NASA launch control procedure, there are numerous engineers whose job it is to call a halt to the countdown if the pressure or temperature they are watching goes beyond some precisely defined limits. However, they can't afford to wait until the limit is exceeded; they must seek to predict if it is likely to go out, particularly during the later stages of the countdown. Of course, this takes more judgment and has greater elements of risk, responsibility, and personal stress than simply waiting for a clear signal of trouble.

Obviously, in highly costly programs, even the subordinates can't afford to wait for a technical process to go "out of limits." Failures must be prevented at all costs. NASA managers appear to suffer no ill effect from having their actions reviewed with substantial regularity, even when there is no evidence of failure. They speak with some pride about having developed "over-the-shoulders management" in which the superior endeavors to guarantee success, not to wait for failure. When everyone knows the costs of failure and everyone is committed to the same goal—and not to individual goals, such as the numerical scores so characteristic of low-level controls—there is acceptance of the need for constant review in the most critical areas. Engineers are not distressed because their superiors are watching their actions, ready to step in should the system show signs of breaking down—they appreciate the need, and even welcome the possibility of intervention.

Sizing Up the Other Organization

Whether the work is being done by a contractor, within another functional group, by one's own employees, or in another part of the organization not immediately accessible to the project manager, there is the constant problem of predicting the likelihood of successful completion. In complex projects, managers learn to expect the unexpected; they realize that what looks good today may be in deep trouble tomorrow, and that highly effective improvisation may be necessary to overcome very serious problems. Thus it becomes important to assess the capability of the organizations that are dealing with the various subsystems, their leadership, diligence, and competence; to ask what those people are like and how they are really performing.

To find out, the project manager and the coordinators reporting to him seek to build a network of contacts within the various organizations whose work will be vital to the completion of his responsibilities. He seeks contacts at sufficiently low levels to provide him with firsthand information instead of information that is highly filtered and refined, and thus deservedly suspect. Many of these contacts will be "worked" daily during critical periods or when the relationships are being established.

Information Assessed

The project manager obviously needs information on schedules and budgets, but he must also collect information on the organization itself. These are the principal questions posed: How energetic and qualified are the managers and their key technical people? How much priority do they assign to this project, compared with other work that may be in process or in prospect? How effectively do they work together, and what kind of support do they usually receive from upper management and service groups?

The frequency of checking can have a strong effect on the amount of information collected. When a manager is concerned about how the work of a subordinate or a contractor is progressing, or when the participants are strangers to each other, he will tend to increase the frequency of checking. From the point of view of the man or group being checked upon, a high frequency of checking communicates lack of trust, and it may also be a material handicap because of the time consumed responding to initiations and filling out reports. Moreover, when an individual detects that information will be used against him he tends to be circumspect about what is revealed. It is easy to get into a position in which the person being controlled restrains the flow of information and the controller is required to keep increasing the pressure required to extract valid progress reports. A dangerous spiral of administrative costs and conflicts can ensue.

This process shows itself most acutely when cutbacks are required, and it is necessary to calculate alternative costs and the impact of various budget amounts on existing programs. Lower echelons have a variety of ways of protecting certain programs by "proving" that any cutback will strike at the heart of their favorites.

With trust on both sides, the respondent is more candid, and less time and effort are required to obtain information.

SENSITIVITY TO SIGNALS

Anyone experienced in R&D work learns not to jump at the first sign of trouble; troubles are endemic to these nonroutinized, one-of-a-kind activities. The question the manager must always ask is: What is *significant* trouble? He is concerned primarily with the kinds of difficulties that the other organization seems incapable of handling with its normal problem-handling apparatus. Put another way, the project manager is endeavoring to assess their reaction to stress situations.

Most managers make the mistake of using "absolutes" as signals of trouble—or its absence. A quality problem emerges—that means trouble; a test is passed—we have no problems. Outside of routine organizations, there are always going to be such signals of trouble or success, but they are not very meaningful. Many times everything looks good, but the roof is about to cave in because something no one thought about—and for which there is no rule, procedure, or test—has been neglected. The specifics of such problems cannot be predicted, but they are often signaled in advance by changes in the organizational system. Managers spend less time on the project; minor problems proliferate; friction in the relationships between adjacent work groups of departments increases; verbal progress reports become overly glib—or overly reticent; changes occur in the *rate* at which certain events happen, not in whether or not they happen. And *they* are monitored by random probes into the organization—seeing how things are going.

In addition, of course, the manager assesses the normal statistical reports on manpower, performance, cost, etc., checks PERT charts, and notes any significant deviations.

FURTHER EVALUATION OF SIGNALS: WHEN TO PROCEED

The project manager has to decide what signals that suggest potential trouble spots are worth following up by further probes. As we have already suggested, a probe is costly in terms of both the time and energy expended on the probe itself and the lost opportunity of pursuing an alternative probe. All leads can't be followed up.

The information he has is usually combined with other information to determine this decision: previous experience with this particular organization, its reputation, rumors in the field, and other data that may be available—labor problems, materials shortages, pending or recently completed negotiations, and the like. Another element in the manager's decision to act or not are the potential losses in future rapport and the drying up of reliable information once privileged information is revealed.

PRELIMINARY STEPS

If it seems clear that a real problem is emerging, the manager who has made the evaluation may do one or more of the following.

1. Alert higher levels within his own management. Frequently the man who makes the observation is a technical coordinator who must decide when the project office is to be alerted.
2. Alert higher levels within management of the group in trouble. Many coordinators have told us that they observe things that local management hasn't learned, and it often takes a good deal of effort to persuade the organization that it has a problem.
3. Undertake further explorations and probings.
4. Alert other subsystems or stages that may be affected if the problem continues.

Timing here is important. Doing this too soon can provide a signal to relax to the other units, and may reduce everyone's effort, particularly when it appears as though the schedule will be changed because of someone else's problems.

NEXT STEPS

So far the manager has contented himself with alerting the various parties affected by the problem—higher levels of his own management, higher levels in the management of the group in trouble and in interrelated subsystems. If the group in trouble seems unable to resolve the problem, the manager has several options: He may increase the pressure on local management; he may urge local management to take specific measures that he believes will resolve the problem; finally, he may attempt to work around the problem by changing the master plan and allowing stage three to begin, even though stage two has not been completed successfully, or he may authorize another and different method for doing stage two in the hopes that one or the other method will work. Both methods involve increased risks and sharply higher costs, but they may save the schedule.

If these efforts fail and the situation still is not "turning around," then the next step is to consider structural changes. Administrative action is apparently not sufficiently drastic to solve the problem.

Structural changes include evaluating other sources of supply, changing managers, renegotiating certain parts of the contract to reflect changes in requirements or capability, modifications of the specifications, and so forth. More modest examples include providing direct assistance to the troubled unit by sending in specialists from the headquarters organization, requiring more or less subcontracting, and the like.

Structural changes should never be contemplated lightly. Most of these actions involve significant changes in cost; they endanger personal relationships, have wide and sometimes unpredictable impacts, and require substantial effort to implement. A prime test of the effective manager is his ability to anticipate most of the potential ramifications involved in any such drastic action.

ASSESSING ORGANIZATIONAL EFFECTIVENESS

Another way of viewing these middle-level controls is that they seek to assess how the organizational system is functioning as a system. They assume that organizational malfunctioning precedes technical malfunctioning; failures in the former are a good predictor of failures in the latter. Let us look at some examples of both the kinds of organizational relationships that can be monitored and their predictive values.

Work-flow responsiveness. Organizationally, this means that managers responsible for adjacent work-flow stages be willing to engage in some give-and-take and be responsive to each other's needs so that there can be swift resolution of difficulties that span two or more jurisdictions.

Unfortunately, it is quite easy for any group to refuse to consider alternatives, unless "bribed" excessively, by mustering a number of reasonable technical arguments. Evidence that a given manager consistently responds to the project office or other adjacent groups with flat refusals is a sign that upper management should give the manager its concentrated attention and intervene directly whenever it becomes necessary.

The generalization is true for any large-scale organization: Waiting to look at results guarantees a kind of "crisis management" characterized by turmoil and high costs in both material and human resources. Every organization increasingly needs good middle-level controls, which by continuously measuring the degree to which the organization is holding together as an organization can pinpoint potential trouble spots before they become serious.

Finally, these middle-level controls, because they concentrate on the total system, concern themselves with integration and coordination. This means that they assess the ability of subordinates, managers, and work groups to coordinate their activities, make mutually satisfying trade-offs, and get the total job done. By doing so, they contribute to breaking down departmental boundaries and help to unify the organization.

Polarization of issues. Human groups obtain major satisfactions and facilitate their own cohesiveness by sharing in a common dislike or even hatred. In highly integrated systems, work-related groups cannot afford the luxury of these polarizations.

This happens in any organization. For example, marketing and production are at each other's throats over their relative balance of power. No matter what problem comes up—even if it is only a trivial request by marketing for an advance copy of production's next month's schedule—becomes part of the struggle: "Do they want that schedule early to use it with top management to hang us? In some way or other are they trying to show us that they have the power to get us to change our reporting system, to show that we have to defer to them?" Polarization means that everything is evaluated in terms of a power struggle and that divisiveness dominates all decisions.

Monitoring headquarters–field relationships. Typically, the program and project manager have a somewhat blurred division of labor. It is easy for the program manager to be either too assertive in project affairs or too distant.

In the division of labor between field and headquarters, it is important for the program manager to act as a buffer between the field-level technical staff and external demands. He should be the one who responds to the questions, criticisms, and pressures of other headquarter's functional and program people, as well as to external political, technical, and economic pressures.

There are several reasons for this. A reasonable amount of risk taking is essential if innovative solutions to both the predicted and unanticipated technical barriers are to be found. An excessively "safe" approach can lead to high costs, delayed schedules, cumbersome redundancy, and uninspired design. This is not to say that field personnel should make imprudent changes, but that long-run success is probably a function of a somewhat protected development environment in which every step does not have to be justified immediately.

This also represents a functional division of labor. Headquarters personnel should have more time; more experience; supplementary resources, such as readily available advisory services; and greater skill in coping with external initiations. Field personnel need all the time they can get for technical coordinational, monitoring, and development efforts.

Finally, we have a good deal of evidence that a durable field–headquarters relationship, as is true of most leadership situations, requires the higher-status "partner" to prove to those dependent upon him that he has the willingness, the power, and the skill to represent them and protect them from external threats. Lacking this, the headquarters manager will find it increasingly difficult to communicate to field personnel and get the responses he is seeking.

CONCLUSION

There is an old theme in economics about bad money driving out good, and social scientists have noted an analogous tendency for easily quantified measures to drive out more subjective ones. The problem in the control area of management is that it is easier to give numerical scores to what we have called high-level and low-level performance. The result is that the manager is induced—or seduced—into doing things that make him and his unit look good, often at the expense of large organizational goals and the larger system.

This is not to deny the usefulness of high- and low-level controls that try to measure accomplishments by comparing cost, schedule, and performance to date with what was predicted or budgeted. Equally important, however, is what these controls fail to do and fail to show. They are misleading as a measure of performance because they assume rigid plans and unified responsibilities, a misconception that is particularly dangerous in an organization in which the nature of the projects insures that unanticipated obstacles will become expected problems on an almost daily basis.

SELECTED BIBLIOGRAPHY

Although we firmly believe that the design and choice of controls are as critical to managerial success as any variable open to the manager's manipulation, there is not a vast literature on the subject outside the accounting field. In other words, there has not been much managerial attention to the organizational implications of control measures.

One of the classic statements on the impact of budget making and budget constraints on managers is the rather old monograph by Chris Argyris: *The Impact of Budgets on People*, New York, Controllership Foundation, 1952. A more recent field study (in the Netherlands) of the relationship of budget making and budget controls to managerial action is G. H. Hofstede's *The Game of Budget Control*, London, Tavistock Publishers (U.S.: Barnes and Noble). Somewhat similar ground is represented in an interesting collection of articles and papers published in William Brun and Don DeCoster, *Accounting and Its Behavioral Implications*, New York, McGraw-Hill, 1969.

The relationship of the controllers to those controlled is the subject of Herbert Simon et al., *Centralization vs. Decentralization in Organizing the Controller's Department*, New York, Controllership Foundation, 1954.

In our own recent study of large development projects we sought to draw the distinction between controls that cause the manager to look inward and protect his own position and those that motivate him to look to the effective functioning of the larger system. See Chapter 14, "Motivating Systems Responsibility," in L. Sayles and M. Chandler, *Managing Large Systems*, New York, Harper and Row, 1971.

VI

Implementing Management Change

THE PROBLEMS of improving the management capability of educational organizations are overwhelming to the neophyte. To the inexperienced eye it appears as if there are literally thousands of new tasks that much be accomplished in concert, as well as the task of maintaining the operation of the organization. Unfortunately there is no way to stop the world, get off, repair our organization, and get back on. Life must continue, and schools are no exception. Boys and girls continue to present themselves each year for our care and nurture; consequently, we must change our management practices in a gradual process. We cannot afford the luxury of doing away with the present system before the new one is operational. Only in very rare circumstances do we have the opportunity to build a totally new management system. There are, however, several useful strategies at our disposal to help manage our educational systems more efficiently.

Bringing about organizational change is concurrently a simple and a complex procedure. Organizations are constantly evolving and changing, whether by design or by chance. The successful manager will make the appropriate changes happen rather than let change control his behavioral pattern. The question is not whether management change should take place, but how it is going to change and how the change is going to be controlled. If the manager is to be the architect of the organization, then he must assume positive leadership. If he is not the designer of his organization, he has abdicated one of his primary responsibilities to outside influences that are making the decisions that are *his* responsibility.

Recently, a large number of environmental factors have precipitated major changes in the management styles of many educational leaders. A moment's reflection produces images of court orders, union activities by both professional and nonprofessional groups, and a host of other political and pressure groups that exert their influence throughout our social fabric. The accelerated, successful attempts of these organizations in changing the management procedures of school systems shows no sign of abatement. If education is to remain a viable institution, the management skills of the educator must be adequately sophisticated so that these forces within our society may be used to the maximum advantage of education, not to ultimately destroy it.

CHANGE STRATEGIES

When an organization attempts to institute management changes, many alternative strategies need to be considered. The most important criterion in considering these strategies is the effectiveness of the change. Almost any strategy is appropriate if it works!

There are three general approaches to changing the management of an organization. Although the general strategies tend to overlap, most of them can be categorized into one of the three approaches.

The oldest method of management change is to change the behavior of the people who make up the organization. Graduate schools of education have used this strategy to improve the management of schools. An oversimplification of the logic is that better-trained people make better decisions and therefore run better schools. It is difficult to find fault with the logic, but a few problems have developed in its implementation.

One of the most severe of these problems is that once an individual has acquired a new management skill, it becomes both a blessing and a liability to him. Other members of his management team view the new skill as a source of potential increase in organizational effectiveness. Members of the peer group also view the new skill as a personal and a professional threat. Thus the person who has acquired this new skill has had his working relationships with his management team significantly changed. Too often the individual possessing the new management skill has tended to revert to his old behavior and ignore the new skills or patterns of behavior to protect his position. This decreases the personal threat, but it also decreases the potential impact of management change within the organization.

If the possessor of new management skills attempts to implement change in the total organization, he finds that he lacks sufficient leverage to get the practices implemented. Too often he has found himself ostracized from the group, and a liability to the organization, and ultimately loses his status. Almost every educational manager knows at least one of his colleagues who moved too fast for his community or his school system and consequently found himself among the ranks of the unemployed.

The strategy of enhancing the abilities of personnel within an organization to improve the management of that organization is viable and especially important on a long-term basis. In implementing management change on a broad scale such as in a state or a nation, it is imperative that each strategy be used to its maximum extent. Personal improvement remains the key strategy to significant managerial improvement in large segments of the education community.

In making a significant management change in a smaller organization, such as a local school system, the probability of success is considerably lessened by pursuing a strategy of improving individual management skills. The problem of turnover of highly talented administrators and the lack of turnover of administrators who have ceased to grow professionally tend to prevent significant changes of management procedures. It is imperative, however, for the beginning educational manager to be prepared with the most effective techniques so that his skills can be used to the best advantage of the organization.

The second of the three general strategies entails working with a small unit of the existing organization and improving its management skills and procedures. The logic is that once the small unit has demonstrated that good things happen to organizations that use good management practices, everyone will want to mimic their activities and share in their success. Some of the same problems are associated with this strategy as with the training of individuals, such as other divisions of an organization will tend to view the exemplary division as both a personal and a professional threat. With this strategy the prospect for success is largely dependent on the interpersonal and public relations of the exemplary group.

The use of examples is one of the oldest teaching techniques, and has been an effective management tool for political and religious organizations.

Although historically effective, the strategy suffers from the drawback of usually requiring a long lead time before the management procedures of the total organization are significantly changed. The long lead time can work to the advantage of the organization in that it presents less of a personal threat to the members of the organization. It also provides sufficient time for personnel to be trained in new methods and procedures. These factors tend to decrease the human trauma frequently associated with change.

The third general strategy begins at the top of the organizational hierarchy. This strategy usually results in the shortest lead time before changes become operational. In addition to insuring the success of implementation by virtue of top management's involvement in the initial stages of implementation, the decision to make the change applicable to all segments of the organization is more easily made. The ready-made decision makes possible more efficient implementation because there is no need to convince other organizational units to adopt the new procedure. Another advantage is that the status and importance of the change are conveyed to the other members of the organization.

By starting with the top management team, the change strategy can be more closely controlled and monitored by those charged with the responsibility for implementation. This helps prevent the necessity for waiting for others to voluntarily change their behavior patterns and significantly decreases the lead time necessary for the change to diffuse throughout the entire organization.

This system of change lends itself to authoritarian styles of management as well as to participatory styles. Care is necessary to avoid the perception that management change is being imposed from the top levels of the organization arbitrarily.

One disadvantage of this change is, because of the short lead time, the increased need for intensive management training, which frequently is not readily available. The short lead time also causes logistical problems in making sure that ongoing functions are adequately accomplished while the new order of management behavior is implemented. This can precipitate personal as well as organizational stress during the change. Probably the most significant danger in using this strategy is the possibility of alienating personnel within the organization by top-level management's imposing change without adequate participation in appropriate decisions by those affected by those decisions.

Implementing management change is a complex and difficult task. The wide variety of strategies available to the manager in themselves result in confusion because of the ever changing, complex environment into which the educator has been thrust. The necessity to improve the management of the educational enterprise is more apparent every day. The educational manager must make his choice of strategy, but most of all he must begin and he must be successful. If the educator wants to change his primary behavior from that of problem solver to that of problem preventer, he must change the management of his school system. The following articles will help him further explore the techniques of implementing management change in educational organizations.

Roger A. Kaufman describes in detail how to establish an accountability system within a school system. His article describes several models that can be used to implement necessary management changes. His easily understood model will provide an excellent base on which to begin management change.

The second article, written by a team of people associated with the American Management Associations, describes numerous techniques to implement improved management within an organization. The detailed descriptions in the article will give the reader the necessary background for implementing change.

Forrest H. Kirkpatrick, writing in the Society for the Advancement of Management journal, describes management-improvement strategies that are used in the industrial world but that are equally applicable to the educational environment.

Effective Managerial Leadership, by James J. Cribbin, describes the different types of leadership behavior that characterize the kinds of management problems discussed in this book. The descriptions will enable the educational manager to interpret how change strategies can be implemented in a wide variety of management environments.

Management of the educational enterprise is a complex and ever changing process. To be effective in this administrative flux, the educational manager must be a continuing student of management. Hopefully this book will serve to whet the reader's appetite and encourage him to continue his study of management. The educational manager should consider course offerings in schools of business as well as schools of education for further professional growth. The rich literature of management should become an important part of his professional reading diet.

To the student of contemporary education, the need for improved management is apparent. The basic concepts of professional management are well documented and proved by experience in both corporate and noncorporate organizations. It is up to the individual manager to use these resoureces to maximize the opportunity for success in meeting the needs of the youth of our society.

Accountability, a System Approach and the Quantitative Improvement of Education

An attempted integration

ROGER A. KAUFMAN

Professor of Psychology
Graduate School of Human Behavior
U.S. International University
San Diego, Calif.

If Lessinger is not the father of educational accountability, then he must be at least the midwife. During his tenure at the Office of Education and following, not only has he assisted in the birth of accountability, but also he has assisted in providing the neonate with tools for achieving a realistic accountability. These tools include (but are not limited to) auditing, system analysis, and the system approach.

Still other tools exist, and are used by those concerned with the quantitative improvement of education. These additional tools include needs assessment, behavioral objectives (or perhaps even better, measurable performance objectives), planning, pro-

Reprinted from *Educational Technology*, January 1971.

gramming, budgeting systems (PPBS), systems analysis, methods-means selection techniques, PERT (program evaluation review technique), and other related network-based management tools, testing, and assessment.

This article intends to suggest an integration model for these tools for the measurable improvement of education, and the achievement of a professional role and responsibility for educators.

Accountability in education is a concept that is *here*. Accountability for *what* is important to determine, lest we are held accountable for variables over which we have no control.

If we educators, then, are going to be accountable, it would be well if we had tools by which we could (1) determine what we will be accountable for accomplishing, (2) determine methods for achieving predictable results, (3) determine methods for deciding among alternatives, (4) determine methods for the management and control of educational operations, and (5) determine methods for ascertaining the extent to which needs and associated objectives have been met.

Following is an attempt to identify various available tools for achieving a "just" accountability, with the proper perspective of values and valuing (Rucker, 1969) and to suggest a relationship between these tools so that educators and partners in the educational process may determine the utility of each for his own program of accountability.*

The primary function of education is to bring about relevant learning, and the primary task of educators is learning management. The learning management job could be conceived as being the planning, organizing, designing, implementing, and evaluation of learning situations and outcomes, and making required, continuing revisions to insure ongoing relevancy and practicality. It is an accountability process.

If the above is valid, then the way in which salient variables and required resources are identified and utilized becomes the critical question for achieving relevant and practical learning outcomes.

It is not uncommon for managers to erroneously start to determine *how* something should be accomplished before *what* is to be accomplished has been adequately identified and defined—perhaps because of a lack of a reasonable, cohesive model for valid eneducational change. Following is a possible *process* model for education based upon a problem-solving referent, suggesting some alternatives for identifying and possibly integrating current thrusts toward the systematic and valid improvement of education.

A POSSIBLE EDUCATIONAL PROCESS MODEL

Process may be defined as the steps or manner in which an outcome is achieved. A product is an outcome.

---

* It is not the intention here to completely detail and describe these various tools, but rather to identify them, provide some references for further study, and hopefully to put them in perspective.

Education may be viewed as a process that provides learners with the required skills, knowledge, and attitudes to be able to survive and contribute in the world to which they are to go when they legally leave the educational agency. In keeping with this process analogy, education may be viewed as the identification and resolution of problems—what should learners be able to know and do when they graduate (or legally leave), and what should be done to provide them with the requisite skills and knowledge? A number of models, not too dissimilar, have been proposed for both education and problem solving. One model, known to philosophers as the "scientific method," basically consists of the steps of problem identification, setting goals or hypotheses, selecting solution strategies, hypothesis testing, evaluation, and revision. John Dewey's suggested problem-solving process was related to this generic process model.

Corrigan and Kaufman (1966) and Corrigan et al. (1969) have suggested a six-step problem-solving model that seems applicable to the management of learning. The six steps are shown in Figure 1. This model has been called a "system approach" to education, representing a closed-loop, self-correcting process for proceeding from identified needs to predictable outcomes. It represents a suggested process model for defining educational accountability and for being accountable.

Other models have been suggested for "systems" approaches, varying from Lehmann's (1968) seven-step model to other models, which frequently start the educational process from varying points of departure (Silvern, 1968; Cleland and King, 1968; Gibson, 1968; Tanner, 1969).

It is suggested that the six-step "system" process model is appropriate for describing the educational management process and that it may be used as a preliminary referent for identifying and integrating current useful thrusts for the quantitative improvement of education.

Figure 1. A six-step problem-solving model for application to education. The six steps are identified, five within the boxes, and the sixth represented by the broken line, which indicates revision as required by performance.

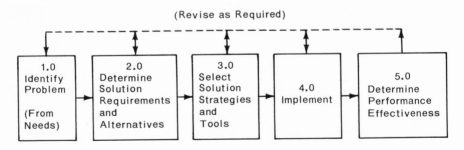

DESCRIPTION OF THE SYSTEM PROCESS

The process model for education indicates six functions, or parts:

1. Identify problem (on the basis of documented needs).
2. Determine solution requirements and solution alternatives.
3. Select strategies and tools (from among the alternatives).
4. Implement.
5. Determine performance effectiveness.
6. Revise as required.

Identify problem. The first step in the suggested process model is to identify the problem(s) on the basis of documented needs. A need may be defined as the discrepancy between "what is" and "what should be." A problem is identified when a particular discrepancy or set of discrepancies has been selected for resolution. The identification of a problem includes the specific delineation of requirements for problem resolution—a definition of required terminal product (or outcome). This step identifies and documents that for which we are to be accountable.

Determine solution requirements and alternatives. After the problem has been identified, an analysis is undertaken to determine the detailed requirements (or specifications) for proceeding from the current condition (what is) to the required condition (what should be). These consist of delineation of overall objectives and subobjectives (products and subproducts) in measurable, performance terms. Additionally, while detailed requirements are being analyzed and identified, possible solution strategies and tools are identified (but not selected) for accomplishing the requirements, including the determination of the advantages and disadvantages of each relative to producing the required outcome(s).

Select strategies and tools. From the alternatives identified in the previous step, criteria for selection are determined, and the selection of appropriate tools and strategies is accomplished. Frequently, selection criteria include cost-benefits or other effectiveness-efficiency indicators.

Implement. On the basis of the needs, the detailed requirements, the alternative ways of getting the outcomes accomplished, and the selected tools and strategies (the ways and means of getting from "what is" to "what should be") are designed, purchased, or obtained, and utilized. This is the "doing" phase, where the actual solution strategies and tools are utilized and appropriate performance data collected.

Determine performance effectiveness. On the basis of the needs and the requirements, the outcomes of the problem-solving process are evaluated to determine the extent to which required results have been achieved. Here the data for terminal achievement (summative evaluation) and for process utility (formative evaluation) are collected, analyzed, compared to requirements, and used to determine revision requirements.

Revise as required. Anytime a performance requirement is not met, necessary revision is required. This critical step insures that a self-correcting process is utilized, and increases the probability of effective and efficient outcomes being obtained. It should be noted that, in the suggested model, revision may be required at any step, or point, in problem resolution—it is not necessary to commit to a "disaster plan" and to have to wait until the plan has been fully implemented to institute required changes.

It is suggested that this process model may have basic utility for the design and accomplishment of effective and efficient education—the first two steps identify the "whats" of problem solution, the remaining steps identify and define the "hows."

CURRENT THRUSTS
FOR MEASURABLE IMPROVEMENT OF EDUCATION

Springing from a number of philosophical and operational sources, several tools have come to the attention of educators as providing rational and realistic ways of improving the educational product.

These include:

1. Needs assessment.
2. System analysis.
3. Behavioral objectives.
4. Planning, programming, budgeting system.
5. Methods-means selection process.
6. Systems analysis.
7. Network-based management tools.
8. Testing and national assessment.
9. Educational auditing.

Each tool seems to hold promise for the measurable improvement of educational activities and outcomes, and for defining and achieving a realistic educational accountability.

Needs assessment. Many educators have become concerned not only with learning but also with the determination of *what* should be learned as a necessary prerequisite to achieving relevant learning outcomes. Needs assessments are formal attempts at determining what should be done and learned in schools. Several school districts are implementing needs assessment, including Newport-Mesa Unified School District and Temple City Unified School District in California, and Mesa School District, Arizona, to name a few.

Needs assessment procedures seem to be keyed to the concept that relevancy of education must be empirically determined from the outset by a formal procedure, which precedes educational planning, design, and implementation (often starting from the identification of symptoms). In most forms, needs assessment identifies and documents the discrepancies between "what is" and "what should be" and provides a valid starting point for education.

System analysis. System analysis is a process for determining the requirements for getting from "what is" to "what should be." As conceived by Kaufman and Corrigan, it consists of analysis, in levels or layers, of requirements for problem solution. They identify the analytical steps of (a) mission analysis, (b) function analysis, (c) task analysis, and (d) methods-means analysis. The outcome of a system analysis is a delineation of feasible "whats" for problem solution, and a listing of possible strategies and tools for achieving each "what."

Behavioral objectives. Usually included in a behavioral objective is the statement of (a) what is to be done, (b) by whom is it to be done, (c) under what conditions is it to be done, (d) what criteria will be used to determine its accomplishment. While most discussions of behavioral objectives are relative to the instruction process directly, the same criteria may be applied to other educational activities as well.

Planning, programming, budgeting system (PPBS). First formally applied to the context of national defense, PPBS represents a powerful tool for educators. In the main, it provides a means for answering questions of education relative to "what do I give" and "what do I get." PPBS identifies the relationships between product outcomes and costs for various alternative methods and means.

Methods-means selection processes. Closely related to PPBS are procedures for deciding among alternative methods and means (strategies and tools) for achieving required outcomes. Briggs *et al.* (1967) offer a test on methods-media selection, and Corrigan (1965) has developed procedures for making effective and efficient media decisions. These methods-means selection procedures are generally based upon the specification of the nature of the learner and the characteristics of available tools and strategies, and the specifications for the learning to be accomplished. Cost-effectiveness is a key criterion.

Systems analysis. Frequently, techniques for selecting among alternative solutions those that will provide the greatest cost-benefit are called "systems" analysis (Cleland and King, 1968). Perhaps the plural form of the word "system" indicates the close linkage with the word used in conjunction with computers and hardware solutions (Kaufman, 1970).

Network-based management tools. Cook and others have introduced the concepts of PERT (program evaluation review technique) and CPM (critical path method) to educators in order for them to better manage and control the educational implementation process (Cook, 1966, 1967). It is suggested that these tools are best applied when all requirements are delineated, the methods and procedures are selected, and the job is to maintain control over the "doing" process.

Testing and national assessment. Testing, of course, is not new to education—in fact most of the major testing tools have been developed by or for educators. Testing provides an understood manner for determining the effectiveness of any treatment, and new tests are being developed constantly. There appear to be, however, some developments in testing that seem to offer promise for educators interested in planned change. One of these developments that relate to measurable performance objectives is criterion-referenced measurement (Glaser, 1966; Popham, 1971), which provides an alternative to norm-referenced tests. Some major testing concerns are, it is understood, developing criterion-referenced testing instruments.

Educational auditing. This concept, which has been explained by Lessinger (1970) is analogous to the certified public accountant who reviews the accomplishments of industrial firms and businesses in terms of expenditures and outcomes. The audit is different from evaluation in that it is oriented toward the statement of accomplishments and does not intend to provide suggestions for revision—it is status- and accomplishment-oriented only. National assessment is now under way, and will provide empirical data relative to how well and how much education is teaching our youngsters (Brian, 1969).

These tools, described all too briefly above, are of interest for a number of reasons: (1) They are empirically grounded, and attempt to quantify that which should or that which is being accomplished in education, (2) they are being considered and in some cases being used by educators, and (3) in some cases they are mandated.

These tools are not unrelated, and following is a suggested manner in which these tools may be related each to the others and to an overall model for the educational process.

AN ATTEMPT AT AN INTEGRATION OF EDUCATIONAL TOOLS

If logical problem solving may be said to follow the above six-step model, then it would seem to be critical to start the process with the advantage of having empirical data to document the problem and its characteristics. Such a beginning referent may be accomplished by an *educational needs assessment*. Such an assessment of needs might well tell us (perhaps only *minimally*) the discrepancies between "what is" and "what should be" so that a valid starting point may be identified.

After a needs assessment has been accomplished, and the specification of the two dimensions of problem solving stated (what is and what should be), further delineation of requirements should be made to determine the subobjectives and requirements for getting from where we are to where we are to be. This analysis may be accomplished by the process tool described earlier as system analysis. The system analysis will provide detailed information relative to solution requirements, and will indicate possible alternative methods and means for accomplishing each requirement. Where instructional programs are being considered, the requirements may be stated in terms of behavioral objectives—learning specifications in measurable performance terms. (For management programs the requirements would be also stated in job performance terms.)

The third function identified in the problem-solving process model is to select solution strategies from alternatives. Here, the basic intent and tools of PPBS and/or systems analysis seem appropriate. On the basis of the data obtained from the needs assessment, the system analysis (and possible statement of behavioral objectives), alternative outcomes and tools may be considered, compared each to the others, projected, and selected. In the case of media, methods-means selection procedures may offer a usable tool for selecting appropriate tools and strategies.

Implementation, the fourth function, is the "meat" of the process, familiar to most educators, and certainly to educational administrators. This how-to-do-it portion is not formally considered here, primarily because it is covered in great detail in texts for schools of administration and management. Tools such as PERT/CPM and other network-based techniques have much to offer the implementer.

The fifth step is "Determine Performance Effectiveness." Here, testing and assessment procedures provide a natural tool for determining how well or how poorly we have achieved our objectives and reduced or eliminated the delineated needs. Evaluation based upon the determined requirements will tend to improve the validity of the testing/assessment procedure. The independent educational accomplishment audit will provide status and outcome data.

By following the functions described in Figure 1, there seems to appear a natural relationship between extant tools for the improvement of education, and for each tool with the overall problem-solving process—a process for defining and achieving educational accountability. Figure 2 graphically presents this suggested relationship.

It should be noted that not all the above tools are completely independent; for instance, PPBS is frequently preceded by system analysis; and frequently, discussion of behavioral objectives includes the requirement for a system analysis and/or a needs assessment.

It would seem to suggest, however, that greater utility may be obtained

Figure 2.   The relationship between current tools for the improvement of education and their relationship with a problem-solving process and a possible model for educational management, and defining and achieving educational accountability.

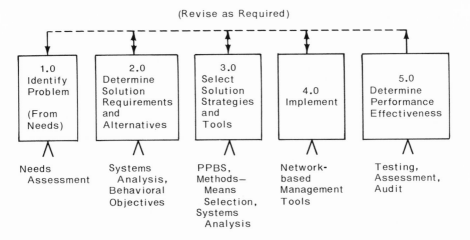

from current statewide and national efforts if each of the "thrust" tools could be defined, and each group working on the improvement of education could work together from a common referent of what is to be done, and how to do it. Perhaps cooperative efforts could provide a single, understandable referent to educational practitioners. For instance, those working on the specification of minimal objectives for high school graduation could obtain data from those conducting needs assessments and system analyses to improve the probability of validity of the graduation objectives (for instance, an objective may be quite measurable and written in performance terms, but be trivial or even wrong!). Those working on PPBS might also benefit from the outcomes of needs assessment, system analysis, and behavioral objectives in order to insure that alternatives being considered are valid.

SUMMARY

The preceding presentation was intended to set a rationale for cooperation and interdependence between professional educational practitioners who are working to measurably improve the products and processes of education and define and achieve a functional accountability. A possible generic model for educational management was presented, identifying six steps for problem solving. Additionally, tools currently being used for the quantifiable improvement of education were briefly presented and discussed.

Finally, an attempt was made to relate the currently utilized tools for the improvement of education with the suggested process model of education, and also relating each of the tools with all the others.

It is hoped that an integration of tools and purposes may be achieved so that education may be aided, in processes and outcomes, by a cooperative, systematic, empirical, evaluatable attack on current and future problems.

SELECTED BIBLIOGRAPHY

BRAIN, G. B. "What's the Score on National Assessment?" *CTA Journal,* May 1969.

BRIGGS, L. J., *et al. Methods—Media Selection in Education.* American Institutes for Research, 1967, Pittsburgh, Pa.

CARPENTER, M. B. "Program Budgeting as a Way to Clarify Issues in Education." RAND Corporation, July 1968.

CARTER, L. F. "The Systems Approach to Education—The Mystique and the Reality." System Development Corporation, SP-3291, January 1969.

CLELAND, D. I., and W. R. KING. *Systems Analysis and Project Management.* New York: McGraw-Hill Book Company, 1968.

COOK, D. L. *PERT: Applications in Education.* Cooperative Research Monograph Number 17, OE-12124, 1966, U.S. Government Printing Office.

———— "Better Project Planning and Control Techniques Through the Use of System Analysis and Management Techniques." A paper presented at the Symposium on Operations Analysis in Education, sponsored by the National Center for Educational Statistics, U.S. Office of Education, November 1967.

CORRIGAN, R. E. "Method-Media Selection." Operation PEP, 1965.

CORRIGAN, R. E., and R. A. KAUFMAN. "The Steps and Tools of the System Approach to Education." Operation PEP, Tulare County Department of Education, Visalia, California, 1966. (A number of documents were produced for Operation PEP and the Chapman College Experienced Teacher Fellowship Program in the area of a System Approach by R. E. Corrigan, Betty O. Corrigan, D. Goodwin, and R. A. Kaufman during the period 1965–68.)

CORRIGAN, R. E., BETTY O. CORRIGAN, D. GOODWIN, and R. A. KAUFMAN. System *Approach for Education (SAFE).* R. E. Corrigan Associates, Garden Grove, Calif., 1969.

GIBSON, L. "Instructional Systems Design Through In-Service Education." *Audio-visual Instruction,* September 1968.

GLASER, R. "Psychological Bases for Instructional Design." *AV Communication Review,* Winter 1966.

KATZENBACH, E. L. *Planning, Programming, Budgeting Systems: PPBS and Education.* The New England School Development Council, March 1968.

KAUFMAN, R. A. "A System Approach to Education. Derivation and Definition." *AV Communication Review,* Winter 1968.

——— "A Management Model." Paper presented to Nova University Conference on Innovations in Education Management, April 1969.

——— *System Approaches to Education: Discussion and Attempted Integration.* ERIC/CEA Monograph, University of Oregon, 1970.

KAUFMAN, R. A., R. E. CORRIGAN, and D. W. JOHNSON. "Toward Educational Responsiveness to Society's Needs: A Tentative Model." Accepted for publication, *Journal of Socio-Economic Planning Sciences.*

LEHMANN, H. "The Systems Approach to Education." *Audiovisual Instruction,* February 1968.

LESSINGER, L. M. "Engineering Accountability into Public Education." Unpublished paper written for Committee for Economic Development, 1970.

——— "The Powerful Notion of Accountability in Education." Paper presented at the Academy on Educational Engineering, Oregon State Department of Public Instruction, Wemme, Oreg, August 10–14, 1970.

MAGER, R. F. *Preparing Instructional Objectives.* Palo Alto: Fearon Publishers, 1962.

PARKER, S. "Planning-Program-Budgeting System." *CTA Journal,* May 1969.

POPMAN, W. JAMES (ed.). *Criterion-Referenced Measurement (An Introduction).* Englewood Cliffs, N.J.: Educational Technology Publications, 1971.

RATH, G. J. "PPBS Is More Than a Budget: It's a Total Planning Process." *Nation's Schools,* November 1968.

RUCKER, W. R. "A Value-Oriented Framework for Education and the Behavioral Sciences." *The Journal of Value Inquiry,* Winter 1969.

SILVERN, L. "Cybernetics and Education K-12." *Audiovisual Instruction,* March 1968.

SMITH, R. G. "The Development of Training Objectives." The George Washington University, Human Resources Research Office, Bulletin 11, June 1964.

SWEIGERT, R. L. "Need Assessment—The First Step Toward Deliberate Rather Than Impulsive Response to Problems." California State Department of Education, 1968.

——— "The Discovery of Need in Education: Developing a Need Inquiry System." *Journal of Secondary Education,* December 1968.

TANNER, C. K. "Techniques and Applications of Educational System Analysis." *Audiovisual Instruction,* March 1969.

U.S. Air Force System Command Manual 70-5, "Work Statement Preparation," February 1, 1968.

U.S. Government, Mil.-Standard 881, "Work Break-Down Structure for Defense Material Items," November 1, 1968.

U.S. Government, Department of Defense, DOD Instruction 7000.2, "Performance Measurement for Selected Acquisitions," December 12, 1967.

A Pattern of Management Action

INSTITUTE MANAGEMENT TEAM

American Management Associations

A. A PROFESSIONAL PATTERN OF ACTION

The lawyer has formulae that guide him in his approach to a case; the doctor follows certain routines in diagnosing an illness; the mechanic has plans by which he inspects his machines; the engineer has definite formulae that he follows regardless of what he is expecting to build. Therefore, it seems reasonable that *a manager should have some simple patterns that he can follow in approaching his job.*

There is seldom much argument with the basic principles of management. The difficulty seems to lie in developing methods by which these principles may be easily applied. Out of an endeavor to solve that particular problem comes a conclusion that we believe leads to a very tangible and definite contribution to the field of management science. Following through on the earlier observation that management is a profession, we suddenly realized that members of other professions have patterns for helping them solve their daily problems.

A professional pattern of action is nothing but a series of steps that have been outlined and arranged in a logical sequence by predecessors in the profession. It tells those who are now in the profession that if they will religiously follow those steps, they can rest assured that they have observed the basic principles of the profession and that necessary factors have been taken into consideration.

Reprinted from *Management of the Educational Enterprise* (Report of the 1971 Institute for Chief State School Officers), Stanford University.

A problem in most organizations today is not to find new things to do, but how to do what is already known to be right. *If we could find a way to put to greater use that which we already know and have, we will have accomplished a great deal.* A pattern of approach should assist toward that end.

It is necessary at this point to make it clear that there is no attempt in this approach to reduce dealing with people to a pattern. *Human relations cannot be reduced to a pattern,* but you can have an orderly approach to human relations problems.

The so-called pattern of management action, outlined in greater detail in the pages that follow, contains eight steps:

1. Plans.
2. Organizational clarification.
3. Standards of performance.
4. Progress review.
5. Action to be taken.
6. Source of action.
7. Time schedule for action.
8. Incentives and rewards.

The pattern itself is the result of asking experienced and successful executives, over a period of a quarter of a century, what, from their experience, they considered to be the most valuable advice they would like to give to their successors. These executives have been individuals engaged in all kinds of organizations and businesses and in some 26 different countries. The number of steps in it and the names of the steps have varied over the years but, basically, the pattern remains about the same and continues to be subjected to the suggestions of successful management people.

The methods by which the pattern is applied differ considerably and change often. However, this pattern has brought about a common vocabulary for terms of management and has established a basis upon which methods may be discussed. It also furnishes a clarification under which the history and research of management can be coordinated and recorded.

It is important to remember that *the greatest value from the application of the management pattern is not the finished work, but the educational processes necessary to securing the finished work.* The discussions involved bring widely divergent viewpoints to a more common understanding. Workers better understand the motives and objectives of their supervisors. Supervisors gain a closer insight into the personalities and thinking processes of their managers. All of this is valuable. The more you direct minds into the same thought channels, the more reasonably sure you may be of accomplishing the objectives of your operations.

The wording of the eight steps is not particularly significant. The terms have been created by supervisors and executives. They have been changed from time to time, but the original significance of each step remains the same.

For illustration, what is now called organization clarification has at various times been called "Job Analysis," "Position Description," etc. What is now called progress review has at various times been called "Rating," "Individual Analysis," "Performance Inventory," "Review and Appraisal," etc. The terms used are not as important as their meaning.

A management pattern puts into the hands of anyone in an executive or supervisory position a series of moves that he must make in order to secure the most desirable action. *It is a method of management.* It is a means of approaching any problem facing an individual who must supervise the activities of others.

A most significant development seems to be the growing appreciation on the part of those following a pattern that it is *a way to diagnose any problem at any time.* Regardless of what the situation may be—an individual management decision or a subject of the agenda for a meeting—the steps of the pattern can be applied constructively for the purpose of insuring a proper decision or solution.

For example, there may be a shortage of supplies. Those involved would apply the management pattern by analyzing the situation as follows: First, is their a known and accepted plan (plans)? Second, is the responsibility clearly fixed for maintaining supplies (organization clarification)? Third, is there any confusion as to objectives (standards of performance)? Fourth, where is the breakdown in the present situation (review)? Fifth, what is needed to correct the situation (action to be taken)? Sixth, who will supply the needs indicated (source)? Seventh, when is action to be taken (time schedule)? Eighth, what is the cost (rewards)?

In other words, the management pattern can be applied to meet conditions as they arise, or on the basis of a logical, comprehensive sequence in an attempt to cover thoroughly all the activities of the business.

Every step of the pattern is now being applied in some way and to some extent by everyone in a managerial job. All a pattern does is to bring these activities together in a simple, logical sequence that acts as a guide and, if followed, insures better attention to the steps involved. It is perfectly logical that the contents of the pattern should not be new because of the nature of their origin. After all, it is simply an expression by successful executives as to the manner in which they work.

1. Plans. Step 1 of a pattern of management action. Every employee on the payroll should know what the overall plan of the company is and what particular contribution he is supposed to make toward its attainment.

In an August, 1968, issue of *Life* magazine is an article, "Montgomery on Rommel." In that article, he tells about the planning and preparation for the battle of Alamein. "My staff entirely approved and worked enthusiastically on the plan . . . one further important point. I was determined that every officer and soldier in the Eighth Army should know the plan for the battle and his part in it. This was done on a careful plan: senior officers first and then down the several grades to the men in the ranks. The latter were told the day before the battle began, after which, no patrols were sent out; I would not risk losing any prisoners to the enemy at this stage.

I reckon the men in the ranks of the Eighth Army knew more about the plan of the battle they were to fight than any other soldiers in history engaged in a major conflict."

A classic story that illustrates the value of knowledge of plans is that of the laborer digging holes. After Joe had been digging in one hole for some time, the foreman told him to climb out and dig one in another place. After Joe had dug to quite some depth in the new hole, the foreman took a look at it, shook his head negatively, and told Joe to start in somewhere else. When this procedure had been repeated four or five times, Joe threw down his shovel and said, with great feeling. "Dig a hole here—dig a hole there—dig, dig, dig! Dig for what? I quit!" The foreman looking at him in astonishment said, "Why Joe, what's the matter with you? I'm trying to find a leak in a pipe line." Joe's face lighted up. He picked up his shovel and went back to work with the comment, "That's different. I'll help."

Another story is told of the typical New York sidewalk-pounder who graces the fences where excavations are made. This particular individual, while draped over a barrier, noticed two men with picks and shovels. They were both working on the same job. The observer asked the first what he was doing. The reply was one that might be expected: "I am digging a hole, what do you think?" He turned to the other fellow and asked him the same question, to which the reply was, "I am helping to build the foundation for a 40-story office building." Here was just a difference in viewpoints, a difference in attitudes.

One of the greatest single influences upon worker attitude is knowledge of objectives—knowledge of what superiors are trying to accomplish—knowledge of the finished product, regardless of what small part the individual may have played in its creation.

2. Organization clarification. Step 2 of a pattern of management action. The term "organization clarification" means that anyone who has supervision over others should make sure that these people understand:

1. What their functions are.
2. What authority goes with those functions.
3. What relationships they have with others.

The activities that must be performed should be carefully and clearly determined. These activities should be divided into organization units and individual positions. Every person in the organization will then know what he is required to do, the extent to which he is to do it, and when he is expected to do it. The activities of each person will be related to each major activity, and individual work can be evaluated according to the contribution it makes to the accomplishment of the major objectives.

Clarification of functions, authority, and relationships is essential to good judgment because such clarification insures proper and complete consideration of the people and the factors involved in a problem. One of the great difficulties in organization is that either the wrong people are consulted or not enough people are consulted in arriving at a decision. There are men who, by intuition, sense the proper people and the proper factors to bring to bear on a given problem but, unfortunately, there are not enough such individuals to go around in an expanding economy.

There is a very simple and helpful device for clarifying *authority*. After each function, include a 1, 2, 3, or 4. These symbols indicate the following authorities for the function:

1. Act.
2. Act and tell.
3. Act after consultation.
4. Act upon instructions from another.

a. *Regimentation?* Organization clarification necessarily means defining the areas in which people work. Some believe this means regimentation. We may as well face that objective and face it squarely. When a plea is made in defense of individual liberty and initiative, it is necessary to point out that an individual who joins an organization must immediately accept certain restrictions that he would not be required to accept were he on his own. Instead of doing what he pleases, when he pleases, and where he pleases, he now must direct his efforts within certain channels. If there are desired activities that organization restrictions do not permit him to perform, he must wait his opportunity through transfer or through proper enlargement in the scope of his work.

When individuals are allowed to follow their own instincts in an organization, their performance becomes unbalanced. They do what they most want to do and what their particular capacities fit them to do, and they devote their entire efforts to these fields. Other responsibilities that good organization demands of the job are neglected. This causes failure in the overall result or necessitates the assumption of these responsibilities by others.

When talking about organization clarification, it is essential to recognize what Chester I. Barnard has so ably described in his book, *The Functions of the Executive.* He refers to the informal phase of organization, which is never clarified or codified. It exists in any organization regardless of how much clarification takes place. It best can be illustrated by stating that if an executive were walking down the hall of an office building and saw a fire in somebody's wastebasket, he would not go by and do nothing about it simply because his position description does not list fire fighting as one of his responsibilities. He would rise to the occasion and do what was required. We, therefore, have both formal description of that which should be clarified, but we still have to leave room for common sense and judgment in relation to things that have not been formalized.

b. *Clarification needed in any organization.* The need for outlining responsibilities, authority, and relationships exists not only in business and industry; it exists wherever you find human beings, regardless of the type of organization.

Does it not seem perfectly reasonable and logical that any individual in any organization should know what he is supposed to do, how much authority he has, and what his relationships are with other people? Does it not seem obvious that to the extent such knowledge does not exist, you will find duplication of effort, omission of responsibility, friction, jealousy, politics, and all the forces that defeat the very purpose of organization?

Such clarification cannot be brought about by wishful thinking or high-sounding philosophies. *It takes hard, careful, well-organized, continuous effort.* It means analyzing an activity from its inception to its conclusion through jobs and departments. It means developing a flow of work indicating who does what, when, and to what extent.

3. *Standards of performance. Step 3 of a pattern of management action. Standards of performance are statements of conditions that will exist when a job is well done.* Each person contributing to the desired result within an organization should have the same understanding of it as all others within the organization.

Can you imagine what would happen in the football stadium or the baseball park if no agreement existed among the members of the team as to the results they were trying to secure? Can you imagine the coach sending the star halfback on the field with instructions to take the ball and run and keep running, paying no attention to the goal line, the stadium, or anything else, run anywhere, run as fast as he can, never stop running? No, the coach does not do that. He tells his backfield to get the ball and make a first down on three tries (not four, because usually you have to kick on the fourth down). That constitutes satisfactory performance. *That is the standard.* If, by chance, the ball carrier can make a touchdown on one try, then he produces better than satisfactory performance and will be recognized for it. While the coach is enthusiastic over superperformance, he will, at the same time, be perfectly satisfied if the standard is reached.

Managers, supervisors, or foremen should have definite objectives for the activities that they are supervising. They should know what constitutes a job well done. They should reduce to writing, for each activity or group of activities, statements of conditions that will result if the work is done as it should be done. It is a pleasant surprise, when starting to work out standards, to see the tremendous improvements that immediately take place. The reason is a better and a more common understanding of objectives.

A great experience awaits the executive or supervisor who calls together his immediate subordinates for a conference to develop standards of performance. In answer to the first question—"What are the major activities of the job that should be measured?"—he will be amazed at the difference in opinions and at the length of time it takes to get agreement.

When an executive then selects one of these activities and asks the question, "What are the conditions that will exist if this factor of the job is well done?" he will be startled at the great variation in answers. Men responsible for the same activities, men doing the same work, men supposed to be getting the same result will have as many different opinions when asked that question as there are men to utter them. It is quite a thrill to see minds finally come together in common agreement upon simple, definite statements.

Does it not seem reasonable that individuals working toward a common objective should have uniform concepts and agreement as to that objective? Does it not seem reasonable that they will work together better as a group and will accomplish more as individuals? Again, standards are not developed by wishful thinking or by high-sounding philosophies. *Patient, continuous, well-organized effort is required to produce the type of standards that will create the attitudes and produce the performance desired.*

Writing a complete set of standards for a job or group of jobs establishes job balance. It gives proper evaluation to the various phases of the job; it focuses attention upon factors of the job that would otherwise be unnoticed.

It is a fairly well-accepted principle that it is good to commend people for work well done. It is all the more effective when such commendation can be given at the time the work is done. This is an extremely important morale-builder. There are practical difficulties, however, that prevent commendation being given as frequently as it should be, or even at the time it should be.

When an individual has standards of performance, he knows what constitutes a job well done. At the end of each day, he knows whether he has done what is expected of him or whether he has exceeded it. Even though his superior may not know it at the time or be anywhere near him—not being able, therefore, to commend him—*he* has the satisfaction of knowing how he stands. He knows that, ultimately, the record will show a satisfactory performance. In the absence of personal commendation, therefore, such realization is, in itself, a morale-builder. Standards of performance perform a very important function in that regard, as well as the other advantage that can be attributed to them.

4. Progress review. Step 4 of a pattern of management action. People in positions of supervision should periodically compare the present performance of individuals under their direction with the standards of performance that have been established. This requires the ability to tell people exactly what you think of their performance and still command their respect and confidence.

This is a most difficult phase of supervision. It is the point at which managers and supervisors analyze the performance of their organizations as compared with the objectives. The work of the pattern up to this point—clarification of jobs, settings of standards—is preparation for this step. All that follows in the pattern is based upon the findings of this step.

This is the point at which "problem cases" must be squarely faced. Many individuals are known to be problems by everyone in the organization except themselves. Attempts are made to transfer our problems to other departments by misrepresenting their qualifications and their performance. *Management cannot and dare not evade individual problem cases.* Neither can it transfer those problems or eliminate them until every possible effort has been made to solve each problem by dealing with it on an individual and understanding basis. It is interesting to note that leaders who have the capacity to discuss the performance of individuals with those individuals themselves, and at the same time create mutual confidence and respect, have few so-called problem cases in their organizations.

a. *Current versus periodic complete checking.* When periodic checking of complete performance is advocated, the reaction is often expressed that "we're continually checking performance. As irregularities come to the attention of the superior, he immediately discusses them with the employee involved." Such comment requires clarification of periodic and complete checking versus current checking as needs indicate. Both are important. One without the other is not always sufficient. Current checking, however, always has been done and is being done. *The contribution that a management pattern makes is a review of complete performance at definite intervals so that the employee may see his own balance sheets.* Continual checkup and careful supervision will always be required. The development of a periodic balanced picture is the purpose of Step 4 of the pattern.

A discussion between supervisor and employee at time of failure is not always sound. Such a discussion may be subject to the emotions of the moment and *when emotions enter, reason exists.* A husband may at some time, for reasons beyond his control, find himself the bridge partner of his wife. He may make some unpardonable error. Comment by his wife at that time is not only discourteous, but may reflect bitterness and may include unreasonable observations. If she would wait until some other time, her instruction would be much more beneficial and social gossips would not have material with which to spread the "confidential" information of a home split by strife and conflict.

Another value of periodic progress review is that *it provides an opportunity for commendation, as well as condemnation.* This seems to be a sound psychological principle. It is not conducive to good morale to "bawl out an individual" for poor performance without leaving that individual with a buildup at the end resulting from expressed hope of improvement or expression of pleasure for some success. When going over the employee's performance in its entirety, *both good and bad performance are discussed,* and some failure that might seem serious by itself may be insignificant as compared with a number of indicated successes.

b. *Confidence in supervisor is important to worker morale.* Good performance and morale require, and are immediately responsive to, a close relationship between man and boss; confidence of one in the other's frank, open, inspirational leadership. A tremendous power in any organization is the feeling on the part of the worker, "I like to work for that man."

Good performance cannot be secured by remote control, by executive order, or by written instructions. It does not exist simply because we think it exists. It will exist only when men and boss are working closely together, and when their thoughts are running in similar channels.

If the executive or supervisory function is to determine what has to be done, to discover how well it is being done, and to develop methods of bringing actual accomplishment closer to objectives, then *this is the point at which actual performance is discovered.* How else can it be done but to check individual performance against objectives?

Many of us have toiled and worried over interpretation of results because statistics have not been adequate or the required information has not been available. If investigation were geared down to each and every employee, we would be much more comprehensive in our analysis and much more accurate in decisions.

Reticence on the part of supervisors and executives to do this individual analysis work has been because of the lack of a proper approach to a very personal situation—the actual performance of a single worker. If functions have been clarified, if standards have been set, then a very simple and sound basis of discussion has been established. Such interviews become less complicated and far more awesome.

The question is frequently asked: Why is there so little contact of this nature between man and boss—why is it so infrequent that a manager will tell the people working for him exactly what he thinks of them in terms of their performance, qualifications, and potential? One reason is that it is one of the most difficult functions to perform. If there is any question in one's mind as to the difficulty involved in criticizing another and still retaining his respect and confidence, a simple illustration may help.

The person who is the closest to a man—who knows him the best and whom he knows the best, and with whom he has the easiest of relationships—is his wife. If there is anyone with whom he should be able to discuss personal matters, it is she. Consider, if you will, the number of times you have returned home late at night from some place you were not expected to be, and what happened upon your arrival at home. Then think of other times when, in the same situation, you thought to yourself on the way home, "This is the time I am going to tell her exactly what I think of her. I am not going to put up with past performance under such situations any longer." Count up the number of times you made such a resolution and then against that, put the number of times you actually did what you resolved to do—and then you know what is meant when it is said that it is the most difficult of human relationships—to criticize another and still retain respect and confidence.

It is easier to do when the preparation for it has been thorough, when you have confidence that your findings are reasonbly fair and accurate, and when you are supported in your opinions by other responsible people.

5. *Action to be taken. Step 5 of a pattern of management action.* Having decided the functions of the job, having decided the results that will be secured if the job is well done, having discovered how well each employee is performing as compared with the standards, an executive or supervisor has the required information *to determine what each person under his direction requires for individual improvement.* That seems to be the intelligent and common-sense basis for a training program. It seems better to base our training courses and our instructional work on the individual needs of the people in the organization rather than upon some fine, beautiful, costly program developed at headquarters that half the people in the oganization do not want

and few need. *If a management pattern has been intelligently applied up to this point, enough individual and group needs will have been discovered for training programs for an indefinite period.*

This particular phase of this pattern provides each employee with a definite program of individual development so that he may perform more satisfactorily and willingly. He is conscious of the fact that his management is trying its best to improve him as an individual and to make him of greater value to society. *This is where the real function of management comes to the front.* A leader is measured by the extent to which he develops those under his direction. This is a morale-builder if ever there was one, and better morale means greater productiveness.

a. *Formal training.* The presentation of a pattern of management action might lead one to believe that formal training is relegated to an area of less importance. *Formal training is more important than it ever was.* However, it is based on this step of the pattern—"action to be taken." The needs for such training are indicated by careful, personal analyses.

Under the old method, there would be a staff of technical experts and editorial writers in a training department who would turn out material. It seems far sounder to refer such requests to the staff department that is dealing specifically with the activity involved. That department should have more information on the technical or professional subject than anyone else. The staff can prepare and edit material and, in fact, it is a basic organization principle that *the staff department should provide the organization with adequate information about its own activity.* If there is no staff department in connection with the activity involved, then some outside agency or specialist may be employed for the assignment.

First, be sure that the formal technical or professional courses are based on the actual needs of the organization; second, that full use is made of the facilities in the organization; and third, that the very finest courses are ultimately developed and supplied.

Since formal training, special technical courses, etc. are practices of long standing in most organizations and have been developed to a high degree, it is not necessary to discuss them here. It is necessary, however, to emphasize that this is the point at which the need for formal training is determined with great care and completeness.

b. *Informal guidance.* While the "action to be taken" normally resolves itself in terms of formal or informal training, a great deal of the action is advice and guidance as to what should be done to solve a particular problem or to meet a job situation. This becomes a suggestion as to what an individual should do or it may become a change in policy, plan, or procedure. It may even take the form of changing responsibility assignment. While this is training of a nature, it is primarily arriving at the solution to something requiring immediate action.

The best formal training methods, conferences, and courses are built around the solution of practical problems anyhow. Much more comes out of review and appraisal than just an inventory of a man. It usually results in a change in practice of some kind or in a change of climate and conditions in which a man performs his responsibilities.

6. Source of action. Step 6 of a pattern of management action. Having determined what action is required as a result of the individual analysis, it is necessary to select the very best source from which to secure it. If the determination of what is needed has been accurate, the same sound judgment can be applied effectively to the selection of the proper persons or sources to meet the need.

Generally speaking, *there are at least four courses of action.* The first is the most important and the others should not be considered until the first has been eliminated.

1. Immediate supervisor.
2. Company specialist.
3. Outside source to be brought in.
4. Outside source to which to go.

The help needed may be for the purpose of changing attitude. This may simply be a matter of contacting certain people or taking part in certain group discussions.

Possibly, greater *skill* or additional *knowledge* is required. This is the point at which participation by staff specialists and department heads may be solicited. It is not uncommon that participation in field activities by a head-quarters staff person is largely due to his own initiative. It is a much healthier condition when his field participation is increased because of invitations from the field.

There are specialists in certain subjects, outside the company, whose services may be secured. *A very thorough investigation, however, should be conducted before any individual or group in the organization receives the help of a specialist.* The specialist must be practical, likable, know his subject, and be able to present it well. In addition, he must be able to adapt himself and his material to the organization.

A very common practice in industry is that known as the educational refund plan. When employees are encouraged to attend outside institutions of learning, companies under such a plan pay a part or all of the cost.

The problem may be one of *habit.* The immediate supervisor is the best possible source of habit-changing efforts. Habits can be changed only through continual coaching, help, and guidance. This comes with everyday supervision.

7. Time schedule for action. Step 7 of a pattern of management action. Definite time should be established for taking indicated action. If all the steps of a pattern have been applied up to this point and definite time is not arranged for supplying what is needed, much may be lost. Here again, the importance of planning must be emphasized. Time does not become available. It must be made available. When *specific periods are set aside for required training and development,* the organization soon adjusts itself to the schedule.

The value of budgeting time should be obvious. Books have been written about it; all kinds of schemes and gadgets have been worked out to assist in it. Still, we do not do enough of it. If time is planned in advance—and well in advance—many of the bridges we fear do not have to be crossed.

a. *Regularly scheduled meetings.* The question always arises as to *meetings.* "We already have too many meetings," someone remarks; "now, we are to have more meetings." It has been definitely proved that if meetings are regularly scheduled and everyone knows that on certain days each week, or each month, he is to attend a meeting, *there are fewer meetings held than when they are called as needed.*

Much of the unfavorable reaction to meetings arises from the practice of notifying people on Friday that they are to be at a meeting on Monday. Confusion is caused, changes in plans are necessary, vacations are interrupted, other people are inconvenienced, the work of the day piles up and is not done. The reaction on the part of the people in the meeting is not favorable. Many of them appear with files of correspondence or memos that must be answered. They occupy themselves with the contents of such material rather than participating in the discussion.

If a salesman, truck driver, clerk, supervisor, or executive knows well in advance that at a certain time he is expected to attend a meeting, he makes no other appointments for that time; he arranges his activities; he provides for the handling of his work; and there is little, if any, disruption of his activities.

b. *Time schedules for individuals or groups.* When, in conducting a review with an employee, it becomes apparent that the help of some other employee is needed, pick up the telephone and make a date in advance. If, in making progress reviews, needs are discovered to be common to an entire group, list the subject on the agenda for a future meeting.

The time schedule takes the form of individual appointments or dates for sessions of the entire group. Experience indicates that as a result of plans, organization clarification, standards of performance, and progress review, enough needs arise to justify the establishment of regular meetings for the group involved.

Regular meetings are set up on the basis of a certan day each month, or twice a month, or each week, depending on the nature of the group and the necessity for group consultation or group help. For example, the executive group meets on the third Thursday of each month. Each member of that group meets with his own supervisory staff on the fourth Wednesday of each month. They in turn meet with their supervisors and foremen on the second Tuesday of each month, until ultimately employee groups are reached, meeting on definite days at a specified time.

This series of regular meetings is known in some areas as council meetings; in some cases, they are lettered for purpose of distinction; i.e., A, B, C, D, etc. In other areas, they are called conferences; in still others, just meetings. Conferences and meetings are identified by names such as, "headquarters management meeting," "headquarters staff conference," "division management meeting," "division staff conference," "salesmen's meeting," "bookkeeping conferences," etc., etc. The whole point involved in this seventh step of this particular pattern of management action is *to set a time in advance for doing what your very careful analysis indicates ought to be done.*

The common sense of such planning seems to be obvious and unquestioned. The difficulty is in training ourselves to do it. If conferences and individual interviews or individual training is planned, if there are agendas in advance, if the people are prepared, if the sessions themselves are carefully and objectively conducted, if careful minutes are prepared, then each session will pay dividends.

c. *Time for contacts outside company.* It was not so long ago that any individual who suggested that a manager might spend weeks off the job for the purpose of receiving further education and training in how to do his job would have been classified as impractical, theoretical, and academic. He even might have been called a dreamer. Today, however, this is a widely recognized and confirmed practice.

For many years, middle management and top-level executives have been taking the 13-week Advanced Management Course at the Harvard School of Business Administration. Smaller numbers have been fortunate members of the Sloan Fellowship Group at Massachusetts Institute of Technology, where they attend for a full year. Other developments are the six-weeks course at Arden House put on by the Columbia School of Business Administration, the Stanford University nine-weeks course, and the eight-weeks course at Cornell. These are just a few, and they are increasing in number all over the country.

In addition, the number of executives who are attending professional conferences and seminars, where they are taking part in valuable exchange of experience and where they are keeping up to date on trends and problems, is increasing by the thousands.

Out of these contacts grow relationships through which individual executives visit companies for varying periods of time in order to find out how they deal with particular problems. Correspondence and telephones keep men up to date with their counterparts in other companies. All this adds up to one of the great dynamic characteristics of the kind of economy in which we live. Our willingness to exchange our know-how with others keeps the whole structure sound.

8. Incentives and rewards. Step 8 of a pattern of management action. Logically, providing for, and timing incentives and rewards, is classified as a type of action to be taken resulting from the progress review. Because of its importance, however, it is singled out and added as another step to this management pattern so that it will not be overlooked, or underrated.

Incentives and rewards are both financial and nonfinancial. The question is frequently asked as to which are the more important. It is very difficult to answer that question because it depends upon certain basic conditions. Until an individual has attained a level of financial return from his work that is reasonably well related to other jobs of similar value, to the standard of living the company expects of incumbents of the job he is on, and to the basic economic necessities of the family he is raising, this type of incentive may be of greater value than the nonfinancial. After he has reached that economic status, even though it may not be as liberal or as high as he could wish for, his interests shift to the work climate in which he finds himself, to the kind of management and associates with whom he works, and to certain job satisfactions that arise from the kind of work he does and how he does it.

There are too many cases of individuals who have refused to take job offers in other companies, where the pay is higher, or who have left a company to join another, where the pay is lower, to underestimate the importance of nonfinancial considerations. At the same time, there have been many individuals who have had to make changes they did not want to make, for no other reason than economic necessity. It is, therefore, difficult to generalize because each case has to be considered in terms of the circumstances that exist.

It is good to be able to report that top managements are giving more consideration to this problem than ever before in history. There has been very full and ready participation in important surveys of executive compensation. Companies are more willing than ever before to exchange information of a very confidential nature in order to secure the benefits of such exchange (AMA's Executive Compensation Service).

The compensation pattern that has been left as a result of the upward squeeze of labor rates is not a good one. The differential between workers and first-line supervision has been radically decreased. White collar workers and middle management people have been caught in an unsatisfactory situation. On top of all this is the decreasing return for high-income executives resulting from the tax burden.

What is important to remember is that if an organization is to be kept high in morale and productivity, and competitive in a free economy, rewards and incentives must be kept adequate to encourage that "job plus" for which America is so famous.

B. BASIC PRINCIPLES AND PATTERNS

A deliberate attempt has been made in the material so far to drive home the realization that the profession of management is based upon certain well-established principles and that their successful application requires some kind of organized, comprehensive pattern of action. In order for a pattern to be adequate to the achievement of objectives, it must provide for the observance of each of the basic principles discussed in [our earlier article]. Thus one way for a manager to check the adequacy of his managerial pattern of action is to go through the various steps of that pattern to see if it has provided for the observance of each of the principles of planning and controlling. If it has not, the pattern is in some respect deficient. It would be helpful at this point to review the eight steps in the pattern just proposed in terms of their attention to the basic principles of management.

Step 1, plans, focuses attention on planning, one of the two basic elements of management. Step 2, organization clarification, establishes procedures and assigns responsibilities, which are two of the requirements under sound planning. This step also provides for the research and information required from which we can determine suitable organization structure, which is one of the media of control. Step 3, standards of performance, supplies objectives, which is another requisite of sound planning. Out of this work both general and specific objectives are secured.

A review of the chart of fundamental principles [see Figure 1] shows that we have now provided for each of those mentioned, with the exception of supervision. The remaining five steps of the pattern—progress review, action to be taken, source, time schedule, and rewards—are all elements of supervision. We, therefore, have provided for the second medium of control.

It would be an unfounded assumption to believe that all the principles of sound management have been discussed here or that all the methods required have been suggested. Experience, however, proves that if just those mentioned are continually kept in mind and the steps of the pattern are continuously and religiously applied, a better type of supervision and management will result than is common in most organizations today. At least, there is less to be left to happy accident of that which executives and supervisors should understand concerning the nature of their responsibilities.

C. FLEXIBILITY

Because we are talking about a planned approach to management responsibility, thereby emphasizing conscious and systematic methods, we are instinctively trying to make this whole presentation exceptionally clear. We have outlined it, have identified specific steps, and have thereby implied a certain order or sequence. Such attempts at clarity and preciseness could lead to an impression of rigidity in application. It is, therefore, necessary at this point to write FLEXIBILITY across the whole management pattern.

While it would be ideal to plan first, to clarify organization, then set stan-

Figure 1

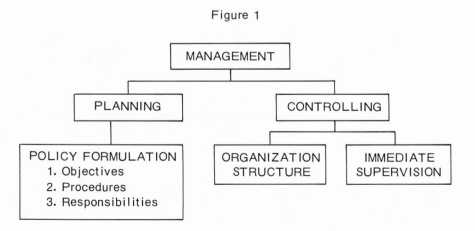

dards, then have progress reviews, etc., it is not always practical or wise to adhere to such a sequence. The use of the steps of a pattern should be determined by the needs that exist at that moment. If the most immediate problem is that of finding out the caliber of people we have and what can be done to improve their competency, then that is where we should start. If we do begin with reviews, without having standards and position descriptions, it will take longer to do the reviews and we inevitably will see the need for and get into standards and position descriptions. The point I am making here is that it is not essential, even though it may be desirable, to take certain steps before you take others.

It is quite possible that the problem in the organization is a lack of clarification as to standards and objectives. That may be what is worrying people more than anything else. You should, therefore, start immediately on the development of standards even though there has been no organization clarification. As you get into standards, it will be discovered that certain organization clarification has to be done. If, however, you go at standards first, the organization clarification work is less difficult when you get it.

A pattern of management action simply lists steps and indicates an ideal sequence. Please do not infer, however, that the sequence has to be followed. Use whatever step is required to meet the most immediate interests and needs of the executive involved. It makes no difference with which step you start: You ultimately will find a need for taking the others.

D. CONSULTATIVE SUPERVISION

The best method of applying a pattern of management action is that known as consultative supervision—getting the full participation of those who are involved.

Set plans with those who have to attain them. Clarify positions with those who are filling the positions. Set standards in consultation with those who have to reach them. Use of the open review is consultation, and the multiple, conference or group review is based upon this principle of consultative supervision.

It might startle some when the statement is made that effective and successful plans for incentives and rewards have been worked out in consultation with those who are to be on the receiving end of such rewards and incentives. One experience stands out clearly in my memory of a special group that was employed by a company to establish a salary and incentive plan for salesmen. This group of experts worked for 18 months and the company spent many thousands of dollars in the development of the plan. The plan was announced, put into effect, and within six months was discarded.

That same company then decided to conduct discussions with groups of salesmen for the purpose of developing an adequate plan. These various groups worked separately at first in the clarification of their suggestions. Representatives of each group then came together in a discussion with representatives of management and, ultimately, a plan was devised and put into effect—the major features of which are still being followed 15 years later.

There is no reason to shy away from the suggestions and ideas of people at lower levels in the organization. It does not make any difference how insignificant or routine a job may be; the person in it knows more about that job and how it should be done than anybody else. The man who is standing at the assembly line, putting nuts on bolts all day, knows more about putting nuts on bolts than anybody else does.

Consultative supervision assumes that responsibility is placed upon individuals—never upon groups. Each individual has authority to make certain decisions and is accountable for the results of such decisions. Before he makes a decision, however, he should consult with anyone who can be helpful to him in arriving at the proper conclusion. When the conclusion is arrived at, he is solely responsible for the results therefrom.

A manager would not be smart if, when consulting with others, they arrived at an acceptable conclusion to him, and he then said, "O.K., we are through talking; I will now make the decision." If he can get others to arrive at conclusions acceptable to him, he should give them credit even though he is responsible for the outcome. He thereby gets their commitment to the successful realization of the course of action decided upon.

Consultative supervision does not call for majority vote or committee action.

E. RESULTS

The practical supervisor will always ask the perfectly logical question, "What are the results from the application of a management pattern? It sounds reasonable, it makes common sense, but is it worth the effort? Does it pay dividends to stockholders, to executives, to employees, and to customers?"

Here are three sources for the answer to that question:

1. The chief executive of the operation, division, company, or organization.
2. The overall results as shown on the balance sheet of the organization.
3. Specific instances.

Those who are occupied full time as staff in promoting the principles of management and in assisting in the improvement of methods receive no formal reports on it, have no responsibility for, and receive no credit directly for specific results. *When a chief executive, individually, or his executive staff, collectively, accept the principles and begin to apply them, it is their program—they operate it, they are responsible for it.*

If a chief executive says the program is good and he expects to continue it, that is the finest report on results we can expect. He knows what is going on in his operation; he knows his expense, his realization, and his volume; if he is good enough to be the chief executive of the operation, he is good enough to judge the value of methods he uses.

One of the best replies to a question on results comes from a chief executive who had been using this approach for years: "You cannot pick out specific results. This program is a method of management. It reaches into every phase of the operation. Look at the overall results of my operation. They are satisfactory, and this program has contributed a great deal toward them."

Specific illustrations are dangerous. Any story of specific improvement implies former carelessness, whereas that is not necessarily true. Such cases, however, are picked up and treated as criticisms. As has been said before, any organization made up of human beings has opportunities for improvement. This helps to discover those opportunities and to provide solutions for them.

Pages could be filled with specific illustrations showing how salesmen have caught an entirely different concept of their relationships with the customer and have not only increased the volume of their business, but the quality of it; how they have put greater volume through fewer and more desirable outlets; how they have reduced controllable selling expenses; how they have improved consumer, public, and organization relationships.

Further illustrations could be given: Clarification of responsibility on expense has saved one operation over $100,000 in one year; improvement in clerical methods has saved one office over $30,000 a year; an office formerly operating from 8:00 A.M. until 6:00 P.M. now operates from 8:00 until 4:00 with the same lunch hour and handles a greater volume of work.

Added to such stories come those of talent previously unappreciated; release of executives with definite skills to other activities, their former jobs being taken over by very capable subordinates. *All of them seem to sum up to increased results at less expense and with better relationships.*

One comment on results is deeply significant and appears in every report written or uttered, and that is—*improvement in morale.* In the possession of the writer are letters from many sections of the world, written by chief executives. The one statement that invariably appears in every one of them emphasizes the noticeable improvement in executive, supervisory, and employee attitude.

After all, improvement in morale is a major motive of the whole program. We repeat again that efficiency as an objective is undesirable, but as a byproduct of good morale, it is a just reward.

Coldly and financially speaking, any management wants greater individual productiveness, but management will get it on a sound basis only through building strong morale, thereby creating in the minds of workers the desire to produce. It seems reasonable to say with deep conviction that the strongest possible morale can be present only when:

1. Plans are motivating.
2. Functions have been clarified.
3. Authority has been properly delegated.
4. Relationships have been clearly outlined.
5. Objectives have been specifically stated and accepted.
6. There is close relationship between supervisor and worker based upon the supervisor's regular and careful review of the worker's performance.
7. Each employee has in his possession a personal development program indicating opportunities for improvement, and a schedule of subjects and helps that has been worked out with his immediate chief.
8. Each is appropriately rewarded when recognition is justified.

When such conditions exist, workers want to produce, and in this case, the term "workers" applies to anybody on the payroll.

Some of us are still idealistic enough to believe that the most routine, monotonous job in the world can be made pleasant by the creation of a situation in which the worker likes his immediate superior, likes his associates, and enjoys the relationships surrounding the task to be done. It seems to be proved by actual tests that the average worker is more interested in the psychological conditions under which he works than in the pay that he receives for the job.

F. MISCELLANEOUS OBSERVATIONS

1. Time for the application of a pattern of management action. People who are already working overtime and who are snowed under with their present responsibilities draw away from the possibility of more meetings, conferences, and other activities required to bring about an orderly, continuous, and conscious method of management. The answer to such a practical situation is faith in the soundness of the approach until proved by action experience.

The best illustration we have is this: You may have been married 15 years ago, bought and moved into a honeymoon cottage that was perfectly satisfactory to meet the needs of the time. Children have come to the home; Grandpa has left this world, and Grandma has come to live with you.

The home is no longer adequate to meet the needs of the family. There is only one bathroom, a small kitchen, an old coal burner in the basement, single-car garage, etc., etc. You have to get up half an hour earlier in the morning to get shaved and out of the way of the children so that they can get ready for school. Literally, you are falling all over each other because the honeymoon cottage does not meet the needs of modern conditions.

You decide to build a new home. While building the home, additional time is involved—evenings, holidays, weekends—you are talking with architects, with builders, selecting wallpaper, hardware, running yourself ragged. Finally, you move into the new home and you find more time on your hands than ever before.

So it is with the application of a management pattern. In trying to clarify your organization, to set standards to be followed, in reviewing performance and supplying needs to improve that performance, additional time is required. *Each hour put into such activities, each responsibility that is clarified, each standard that is set, each improvement in individual performance saves time.* Finally, you discover that you and others in the organization have more time on your hands than you had before, and the entire operation is running much more smoothly.

2. Men and machines. A pattern of management action, as has been stated so many times, is an organized, conscious, and continuous method of management. Frankly, *it is an attempt* to apply to men the same careful consideration that we give machines.

If a company proposed to purchase a new piece of machinery involving capital expenditure of about $50,000, what would be the company's procedure?

It carefully would determine what the machine is to do (its functions), and learn its production capacity (standards of performance). If these seem to be reasonably sound and the money is available, the machine would be purchased and installed. Periodically, an inspector would check the machine (progress review); from his report, it would be determined what the machine needed in the way of repair, maintenance, or replacement (action to be taken).

A decision would be made as to the best *source* for having the work done. Can the operator do it? Is the shop mechanic the man to do it? Should it be taken to the plant shop? Should some mechanic from outside be brought in? Or, should the machine be sent back to the manufacturer? The best *time* to do this work would then be determined so that provision could be made to reorganize the work in the shop in order to pick up the slack while the machine is out of production. Then we would determine the cost (rewards).

Does it not seem reasonable that *we should apply the same care and the same logic, the same intelligence, the same consideration to the man who operates the machine as we do to the machine itself?* We have a larger investment in the man; we have a greater potential in the man. The whole professional management program is simply an appeal to the common sense, to the sound reasoning of the executive and supervisory staff, in an effort to impress those involved with this logic.

G. An Important and Basic Principle

In applying management techniques, it is imperative that we keep the techniques in proper perspective. No manager should develop any fondness for a technique in itself. I do not know of any manager who is devoting much time to the collection of plans just for the sake of having a collection of good plans. (Libraries and researchers, yes, but not managers.) I do not know of a manager interested in collecting position descriptions for the sake of having position descriptions. Managers should not be interested in the development of perfect standards of performance just for the sake of attaining perfection in that medium. What *is* important is the process of applying the technique—the process of bringing a supervisor and a subordinate closer and closer together in their mental images of what is to be done and how well it is to be done.

THE VALUE OF THE USE OF A MANAGEMENT TECHNIQUE IS THE IMPACT IT HAS UPON HUMAN PERFORMANCE. This is the prime reason it is important that managers use these techniques in working with their people.

At a time when managers are concerned about inflation and wage and price controls, it is appropriate to give attention to what can be done to increase efficiency, improve operations, and "sharpen our competitive edge." Can these improvements be accomplished unless we make some changes in the functioning of people who are performing the various tasks of management?

New Dimensions in the Management Function

FORREST H. KIRKPATRICK

Vice President (retired)
Wheeling-Pittsburgh Steel Corp.
Wheeling, W. Va.

Matters related to efficiency, improvement, and competition have always been considered part of the management function, but so often any action related to them has been handled according to "standard operating procedure." But today, when pressures are increasing and competition is more and more persistent, it is well to take a new look at what has been done and what can be done to add some new dimensions to the management function—and specifically to "manage" for improvement and increased efficiency.

First of all, this means that "improvement" must be considered one of the most important functions along with planning, organizing, operating, and controlling. Competition, the greatest single stimulant, is a constant reminder that those who do not work toward improvement are, in fact, working toward oblivion.

Most management men—at every level—declare that they are "for" improvement. They go on to show why by enumerating such reasons as survival, growth, progress, and such personal considerations as advancement, development, and prestige. On occasion I have asked people in management responsibilities how they feel about this part of their job and a composite answer would read like this:

Reprinted from *S.A.M. Advanced Management Journal,* January 1972.

We are in favor of improvement and increased efficiency and we have it constantly on our minds. . . .

But, when you go on to inquire of these same men what specifically they do, day in and day out, as part of the management function, they answer: directing, coordinating, appraising, conferring, listening, delegating, controlling, encouraging, selling the company, creating goodwill, and the like, Rarely do they mention "improvement" as a major concern of each day. It seems to me that it is never quite at the top of the list—and sometimes not in evidence—as an important function.

Partly reflecting the changes in times and in their own thinking, management men thoughout the course of history have employed a variety of motivation techniques related mostly to production, viz:

1. From the ancient and long-held concept of "we'll make them do it" there have emerged at least three practices: force, fear, and that combination of the two known as authority. The combination of force and fear found in the authority of rank and position has been the mainstay of management men in the long sweep of military and business history.

2. From a more modern concept of "we'll make them want to do it" have emerged at least two techniques: persuasion and rewards. Persuasion involves convincing and selling. Rewards combine the process of persuasion with the added note of recompense in some form.

3. A comparatively new concept of "we will make certain the job has many satisfactions" is being tried and recommended as more effective and more appropriate for many situations—perhaps for all. Related to this concept is the recurring reminder to management men that they get results through others.

Everyone recognizes that authoritative management has been somewhat effective with respect to many areas and situations, but in the area that might be called "sharpening the competitive edge," that is, the area of creating improvements, people just do not respond to that technique. Any improvement may tighten down the screws of performance and cause reactions. Endless examples might be cited in which even moving in the direction of an improvement procedure has resulted in resentment and insecurity—sometimes to the point where employees involved were characterized as unstable, irksome, or perverse.

Managers cannot be blamed for wanting to avoid such reactions as much as possible, but I would remind them that it is a mistake to assume that resentment is a necessary concomitant to improvement. Under certain conditions people do not react negatively to the idea of improvement. Both individuals and groups have demonstrated that, given the right atmosphere and opportunity, improvement is not a perplexing and difficult problem.

When a man takes a job, he enters into a kind of "social bargain" with other people. The social scientists might spell it out this way:

No man exists as an isolated individual. He enters every situation subordinate to some and superior to others. While other people are satisfying their normal human drives through him, he is at the same time satisfying his drives through them. In effect, he makes a bargain with others—work associates, employers, yes, parents, wife, children, friends—to obtain as much satisfaction as he can, while not interfering with their own satisfactions.

Essentially, then, here is part of the problem of personal freedom—its use and control. A man needs freedom to satisfy his drives, but he must give up some of his freedom to others. The character of the bargain that he makes with others is always measured in terms of the satisfaction it does or does not provide.

If the bargain a man has made with his company or firm involves, among other things, a dependable adherence to the pattern and procedures of the situation, and this is the condition that has previously provided satisfaction to both manager and the managed, then any change or any attempt to change will interfere with this condition. In a sense, this means that the old bargain is broken and a new bargain is in the making.

One can well understand, therefore, why we often have personal adjustment problems in effecting changes in procedures and operations. This is the time also to point out that motivation arises from mutuality of interest. Where the interest of the manager and the managed are the same, then, there are no situations wherein people work listlessly and incompletely.

The various other techniques of motivation—authority, fear, persuasion, rewards, and satisfactions—may have their place, but only as they can be related to the unsatisfied drives of human nature. For example, fear of the loss of the job through fear of the boss means little compared to being found incapable of group action or acceptance in a situation, or being unable to learn and develop.

Our insights—as well as our techniques or procedures—related to motivation are still very limited. Certainly pep talks, slogans, and gimmicks have little to do with moving people toward more work or better performance. It is appropriate, therefore, as we think about the management function to ask the $64 question. In the light of the contribution of social science to our current knowledge about human behavior combined with day-to-day observations, what changes should we recommend?

We can begin with the idea that a man puts more emotional and psychic energy into a project that satisfies him deeply—a project whose appeal touches as many of his needs and aspirations as possible. The key, of course, lies in finding the aims of the person. An appeal to personal aims is often the most effective. Those often center around the employee's growth and development, his creative and improvement potential, his wider scope of responsibility. The manager should know this because it is also true of him.

What we might call "managing for improvement" is about the same at all levels of responsibility. The differences are principally of degree and of interrelationship, and they do not affect the three main requirements for action, viz:

1. Managers must develop and maintain a constant concern for increased efficiency and improvement.
2. Managers must next find procedures to implement this attitude in everyday practice.
3. The final step in the process is the implementation of a step-by-step program—designed around communication and motivation—with action as the chief ingredient.

Management performance has been most satisfactory when managers were close to their people and when they gave continuous evidence of understanding their interests and the relation of these interests to their work. This is the essence of good communications. Bigger and better company newspapers, bigger and better bulletin boards are not the answer. There must be a striving for mutuality of interests that goes deeper than the obvious. Managing with this kind of consideration, understanding, and sensitivity is not new; it has been going on for years.

As of today, we are likely to find management somewhere along the line of three levels of growth in its groping for these new dimensions.

1. *Participative management* is the stage of allocating a portion of the management function to the managed. In practice, this involves seeking suggestions and ideas in recognition of the simple fact that many of our associates do have intelligent and constructive ideas. The project team is the usual form of implementing participation on a group basis.

2. *Consultative management* is that stage of granting a share of management to the managed. In practice, this is an enlargement of the concept of participation, the principle that people will be consulted in all matters that are of concern to them. The group is given a designated share of the management function as its continuing responsibility.

3. *Responsive management* is that stage of seeking a genuine rapport with management. This kind of management is still too new even to be defined fully, but it seems to be the course progressive enterprises will try out. This level will probably be more and more implemented around a leader, dealing directly with individuals and groups as they work out the total management situation together. What the ultimate organizational structure will be is open to question.

My observations are, of course, suggestive and not specific because in each situation there will be great differences in implementation or application. It is clear, I am sure, that I am discussing new dimensions in the management function that are related to personnel utilization in its best sense. That kind of philosophy—if we can call it that—will undoubtedly change the functioning of managers in many of their customary activities—delegation, for instance.

Traditionally, delegation simply involved giving a job to one man who was equipped to perform it, and he as the specialist accepted direction and control as part of authoritative management. With the advent of these new dimensions, more delegation will progressively be made to groups, with the total responsibility for the complete task being apportioned among the group members.

To be more specific about "improvement," the central theme must be a methodology that is systematic and direct—in the true management sense. This approach consists of five major steps that should be useful for individuals and groups alike as we try to move toward our objectives, viz:

1. *The situation.* This is the descriptive step in which we describe the situation before us—by reporting the pertinent facts, by gathering the appropriate data, by stating the surrounding conditions. This establishes the framework of our difficulties.

It is typical to think in terms of the specific problems as contrasted to the whole situation. It is important that we orient ourselves toward the total situation, rather than toward one particular problem in order to avoid making a flash decision as to what the problem is.

2. *The problem(s).* This is the analytical step in which we specify the problems represented by the difficulties of the situation. In addition, we determine the priority of attack on these problems.

3. *Possible solutions.* This is the thoughtful and creative step in which we accumulate all the many and varied possibilities for handling the problem. There are two dangers to watch for at this point. The first is the enthusiastic flash decision that selects the first creative notion and seizes on it as the final answer. The second—even more deadly—is the introduction of evaluation. The creative process will be killed by criticism that is designed to evaluate or judge an item offered as a possible solution. (Such judgment is strictly reserved for Step 4, the determination of the preferred solution.)

4. *The preferred solution.* This is the judicial step in which the possibilities are evaluated and arrayed in an order of preference. Several years ago, I learned of a concept titled "differential analysis." This calls for maintenance of an element of flexibility by recognizing that the management situation is dynamic and changes in it may well influence any final decision; in other words, the preferred solution is never black or white.

5. *Plan of action.* This is the projective step in which the preferred solution and alternatives to it are visualized in terms of the overall situation from which the problem arose. At this point, a course of action should be recommended in as much detail as may be needed to make it effective.

All managers must also be willing to try something that may not work. This research attitude will serve to encourage creativity by furnishing more opportunities for testing recommendations. Neither the manager nor the other persons involved may be truly able to encompass the full range of responsibilities without trial runs, models, or whatever may be needed to work out the bugs or to find the facts. This attitude of experimentation provides the climate for creativity as well as the safety valve for ideas that otherwise might never see the light of day.

Nothing will serve as a greater deterrent to the effective implementation of improvement than a disease that might be called "motor mania." The symptoms of this condition are that we never have time to reflect, time to think through a problem; we cannot explore or examine; we do not dare relax; and we are always in motion. Motor mania is second only to lack of management interest as a cause of the downfall of any improvement program.

Every manager knows that there is endless opportunity for improvement in every work situation. As he advances toward the stage of what I have called responsive management, he will find that his associates will want to establish lists and priorities of possible projects and to set goals of attainment. His acceptance and publication of these lists and goals, together with some indication of the more valuable areas, will provide support and encouragement for an improvement program that will be active, vigorous, and rewarding.

Techniques, procedures, tools, mathematical models, manpower charts, and all the rest are important as we move toward keener competition and greater efficiency in each firm—and in the overall economy. But beyond all these, we must ultimately think in terms of improving the effectiveness of all those involved in the management function. The human factors, the emotional factors, and the interpersonal relations factors are new and important dimensions—and these need to be explored and exploited in the functioning of management.

There is no way to set aside the fact that the manager sits at the center of the maelstrom. His desk is the final destination of the briskly passing buck. He has one full-time job trying to keep track of what is happening and another full-time job trying to control it. Conditions that once could be relied on to remain substantially unchanged for ten years are now beyond recognition in a few months.

In summary, management men frequently ask what are some of the most significant principles and truths that have emerged from the search for better management procedures—for the new dimensions. My answer to that query will probably change from year to year, but, as of this moment, the following seem to be the ten most important commandments for people who are engaged in top management responsibilities:

1. Identify the people of an organization as its greatest asset.
2. Approach every task in an organized, conscious manner so that the outcome will not be left to chance.
3. Establish definite long- and short-range objectives to insure greater accomplishment.
4. Secure full attainment of objectives through general understanding and acceptance of them by others.
5. Keep individual members of the team alert and ready by seeing that each one knows what he is supposed to do, what his authority is, and what his work relationships with others should be.
6. Concentrate on individual improvement through regular review of performance and potential.

7. Provide opportunity for assistance and guidance in self-development as a fundamental of institutional growth.
8. Maintain adequate and timely incentives and rewards for increase in human effort.
9. Supply work satisfactions for those who perform the work and those who are served by it.
10. Make adequate profit in order to continue to keep alive and render service.

I shall close this article by passing along some homely and very practical suggestions for the manager's own personal career, viz:

1. *Keep your eye on the clock.* You cannot see it, you cannot touch it, you cannot package or bottle it, yet time is one of the most valuable resources at your command. Managing time takes several forms. It involves first of all evaluating all the things that might make a claim on your time—and deciding how much time each is worth. Some are not worth spending any time on at all. And others are worth a great deal. And so we set priorities—as to amount of time we allocate, and what we do first, second, third.

2. *Multiply yourself.* You will find that when you delegate—when you push every job as far down the line as possible—you do several things at once. You free yourself to do the things you should be doing that the others cannot do, and by letting the others stretch themselves, you find out which ones are dependable and ready.

Delegation is not an escape hatch for the lazy or timid. On the contrary, it is one of the most challenging responsibilities of any manager. It requires intelligence to determine just how much should be delegated and to whom. It takes imagination to visualize the scope of delegation and under precisely what conditions it can best fulfill the goals you are striving for. And finally, it takes courage. It is not easy to trust someone else with a job for which you will ultimately be held responsible.

3. *Pick quality.* I have seen men who hesitated to hire, recruit, or promote another man because they were afraid he would create competition for them. This is unwise and dangerous. In a going concern, a man may pass you for a particular position. But he will not keep you from moving up, maybe even passing him later.

Quality people are not simply 20 percent or 30 percent better than mediocre people. I think they are more like 200 percent or 300 percent better. They actually outperform the others by that kind of ratio. And, as Robert Ingersoll said, "The superior man rises by lifting others." This means that he contributes to an environment of excellence.

Quality people are tough to get, tough to manage, and tough to hang onto. They make you run harder and faster. They push you, make you stretch. In short, quite aside from their contribution to the corporate effort, they're the best thing in the world for you.

4. *Hold to high standards.* Excellence is the only alternative for mediocrity.

There is no room for compromise. The greatest enemy faced by any manager is mediocrity. It is born with the comment, "Look—this is good enough." Demand excellence of yourself—of your subordinates, associates, and superiors—and of your organization. And expect them to demand the same in return.

It is well known that the more talented employees respond well to high standards of performance. In periods of high employment and high turnover, many managers become timid about demanding top performance. "If we're too tough, we'll lose them," they say. The fact is, that is not what happens.

5. *Let them run.* If you have picked quality people as much as possible, let them run on a track of their own. In any organization, large or small, the forward thrust, the creative ideas, the real push often come from the younger people who are trying to make their way to the top. It becomes forward thrust, of course, only if the people at the top are receptive—if they maintain a climate where creative ideas are welcomed and tried out.

I do not pretend to know much about how companies get themselves rolling. But I do know this much. It starts with individuals—people who are constructively restless and ambitious. And I know that this kind of spirit is contagious, that the carriers of this contagion are among the most valuable people in the organization.

6. *Don't alibi.* If I were to pick a single personal quality that has characterized every man I have seen go to the top, it would be that he was, first and last and above everything else, a man of inner integrity.

When things got tough, when the going got rough, he stood up to it. If things went wrong under his direction, he did not make excuses. He just went on from there.

Think how rare is the man who says, "I was wrong," and how much you have respected the man who said it. These are the big people that you see at the top or on their way up.

7. *Keep in touch.* In other words, communicate. And do it with your ears as well as your mouth. In fact, we should remember that the good Lord gave us two ears and only one mouth. Use them in that proportion. And when you do talk with your people, do it affirmatively, not defensively—for what it will do positively for their morale, their productivity, and their overall effectiveness.

People want to know several things. They want to know what their own job is all about, why they are doing what we ask them to do, what good it does anybody, and above all how well they are doing it. And then they want to know what's going on—if they see strange things happening, or hear rumors that something new is about to happen, they want to know about it.

8. *Don't forget yourself.* There is a charming little story about a Japanese artist who painted a picture on a fairly large canvas. Down in one corner was a tree and on the limbs of the tree were some birds—but all the rest of the canvas was bare. When he was asked if he were not going to paint something more to fill in the rest of the canvas, he said, "Oh no, I have

to leave room for the birds to fly." So often we fill our lives so full that there is no room for the birds to fly.

Have outside interests, for a change of pace. You will profit and so will your family. And so, in fact, will your associates, for you will develop a more balanced and broader perspective.

But know your limits—and stay within them. Don't take on more than you can do well. Remember—you can't run your job from a hospital bed . . . and it's impossible to be a success in the cemetery.

Fifty-seven Varieties of Leader

JAMES J. CRIBBIN

Professor of Management
Graduate School of Business
St. John's University
Jamaica, N.Y.

An annoying aspect of managerial leadership is that the phenomenon is readily observed in any organization; yet how one becomes a leader defies precise explanation. Some people have a knack for assuming a leadership role and being accepted and followed by a group, whereas others would have difficulty leading a horde of hungry orphans to a hot-dog stand. There is no science of leadership; there are no prescriptions that will guarantee success in influencing others, no formulas that can be followed. To make matters worse, at times even the most unlikely people seem to achieve a leadership status. Leadership is more an art than management itself. Thus the dilemma remains: Leaders abound; explanations of how they attained their position elude convincing analysis.

In the face of such frustration, it is not surprising that authorities have been tempted to construct managerial taxonomies. Certainly they have not lacked imagination in conjuring up descriptive terminology for various sorts of leaders. Terms like "democratic" "impoverished," "task-oriented," "manipulative," "psychologically distant," "custodial," "free-rein," exploitative," "autocratic," "missionary," and "nondirective" fill the literature. Each writer not only seems quite content with his own nomenclature but tends to ignore those of his peers. To help the executive thread his way through the maze, here we will consider some of the more rhetorical descriptions of leaders.

Reprinted from *Effective Managerial Leadership*, Chapter 2, AMA, 1972.

FORMAL VERSUS NONFORMAL LEADERSHIP

Any company can be considered an arena in which the organizers meet the organized. To insure that its objectives are attained, the firm appoints formal leaders, who are given the right to direct and control the activities of subordinates. They are vested with the authority to carry out their functions and duties. By and large, they execute their responsibilities through the mechanisms of the organization structure. They are readily recognized from their titles, their status, and the way they are treated by subordinates, at least in public. Not too surprisingly, the organized often muster their resources to safeguard what they consider to be their legitimate rights, needs, and wants. Quite apart from, or indeed in spite of, the wishes of higher authority, the work group often *silently selects* and *silently elects* other leaders. To them it looks for guidance; from them it accepts direction.

One day a consultant doing some work for a firm asked a certain vice president's secretary if he was available. "Why do you want to see him?" was the rather surprising reply. "Among other reasons," replied the consultant, "because he is a vice president." She smiled and answered, "Oh, no. He's the president's brother-in-law. If you really want to know how things are done around here and what's going on, talk with Mr. X. He's the one everybody turns to for help."

This incident illustrates the fact that the manager does not become a leader because he occupies a given niche in the organization totem pole. Until he wins his spurs with the group, he may remain a merely nominal leader, a figurehead or position holder. Although it is popular to speak of the so-called informal group, there is little that is informal about it. A better term is *nonformal,* since such a group is not recognized by higher management. Nor, of course, does it fit into the formal organizational structure in any rational or planned way.

This divergence of values and views between the organizers and the organized can at times place the manager in a rather uncomfortable situation. He is supported by the firm, which charges him with welding a team out of mismatched parts, people whom he has inherited, selected, or had imposed on him. The nonformal leader, on the other hand, has the support of the work group. The manager or supervisor has the twin task of satisfying the rightful demands of the organization while helping his people satisfy their needs and aspirations. The nonformal leader seeks only to help his followers achieve their personal and group goals. As a result, the manager or supervisor in a very real sense can end up as the man in the middle of two opposing forces. What can he do in such a situation?

He must simply accept the fact that his *legal* right to manage others does not qualify him to lead them. He must earn a *psychological* and *sociological* right to do so. Influence is merited and gained, not coerced and demanded.

He can prevent his own insecurities from compelling him to look upon the nonformal leaders as the enemy. Companies at times make this mistake in their promotion policies. Instead of seeking out, winning over, and advancing the competent natural leaders, they pick men who are more docile and less troublesome. The drawback of such an approach is demonstrated by a study showing that union people who were made supervisors tended to develop both promanagement and contraunion attitudes, whereas those who were elected shop stewards became more prounion but not more antimanagement. If the supervisor or manager has negative or jealous feelings toward the nonformal leaders, it will be difficult or impossible for him to relate to them in any constructive manner.

Barnard pointed out long ago that the existence of nonformal work groups was a natural and inevitable phenomenon and generally a healthy one, since they helped the formal organization adjust to changing corporate realities. In a word, nonformal groups often make the organization work in spite of its built-in rigidities. If the manager can accept this as a fact of organizational life, then he can evolve tactics for cooperating or at least coping with a group's chosen head.

Nonformal leaders derive their positions from various strengths: They are the natural leaders; they often represent and verbalize the real feelings and reactions of the work group; they can color the group's thinking and attitudes; they can help to hinder management's plans or procedures; they are at times key factors in the communications network since people depend on them for a straight story; they can more often than not provide rewards and punishments that may be more compelling than those offered by the department or firm.

Since few if any managers or supervisors can become the nonformal leaders of their work groups, the would-be manager–leader should study his nonformal counterpart to ascertain the role he plays as far as the workforce is concerned. After all, the nonformal leader is a result, not a cause. The more the officially designated leader can help his people attain their goals through the organization, the less they will need to turn to the nonformal leader.

The manager should do his best to build a relationship with the nonformal leader based on mutual respect and consideration, avoiding the two extremes of giving the company away in petty private deals and of fighting him tooth and nail. It is pitiful to see some supervisors and managers bending their efforts to increasing the psychological and sociological distance between their employees and themselves instead of seeking to interact with them and help them identify more fully with the company or department.

AUTHORITARIAN, DEMOCRATIC, AND LAISSEZ-FAIRE LEADERS

A man is both the beneficiary and the victim of his culture. The social milieu in which he lives and has his being exerts a powerful influence on his values, perceptions, and attitudes. It is not surprising, therefore, that about the time of World War II, the public began to pigeonhole leaders as democratic, autocratic, or laissez-faire. The successes of fascism terrified the world; the upsurge of antihumanistic political philosophies stunned it. Centuries of painful effort to protect and extend human rights were in danger of being wiped out by a Cro-Magnon concept of man and freedom. In such conditions, it was inevitable perhaps that the authoritarian leader was considered a child of darkness, the democratic leader a child of light. The former was doomed to being perceived as self-insistent, dictatorial, harsh, punitive, threatening, power-conscious, restrictive, and all too eager to seek out scapegoats; the latter was seen as egalitarian, facilitative, group-centered, permissive, participative, responsive to the needs of his followers, and geared to consent and consensus.

There is considerable evidence that a so-called democratic leadership style has many advantages over an authoritarian one and *under certain conditions* can yield rich results; this is not the problem. The real difficulty is that dividing all leaders into three parts, like Caesar's Gaul, is a bit too pat. Democracy per se has nothing to do with leadership in business and industry. It is a political philosophy or a commitment to a way of life that is supercharged with emotional allegiances. Autocracy has the converse hypersensitive aura. The tenor of the times was such, however, that democracy was purported to be inevitable in the modern firm. This may be a laudable, even desirable goal. But the simple fact is that for the foreseeable future it is more a holy grail than a practical strategy that will enable the general run of executives to improve their leadership behavior on the day-to-day job.

Robert McMurry and Eugene Jennings, authorities who would yield to none in their loyalty to the philosophy of democracy, affirmed that in certain situations there might well be a proper place for the directive type of manager–leader.[1] For the most part, however, theirs were small voices that were drowned in the emotional winds. In retrospect, the whole labeling process was somewhat self-defeating. In a democracy, it is clear, the good guy with the white hat will be a democratic leader, and the script will call for the authoritarian manager to end his days wearing a black hat. Unhappily, in an autocratic philosophy or climate, the reverse will be true. Neither approach lends itself to a clearer understanding of the subject. It is perhaps prudent to lay to rest views of the leadership process in business that have their roots in highly emotional political convictions.

LEADERS IN BUREAUCRACIES

In an engaging book, Anthony Downs describes bureaucratic leaders in eye-catching terms.[2] He divides them into climbers, conservers, zealots, advocates, and statesmen.

Climbers, as the name implies, are self-propelled in their quest for ever increasing power and prestige. They are sensitively opportunistic in seeking out avenues for personal progress and self-aggrandizement. Weaker managers feel their aggressive strategies. Departments whose resources for resistance are low are likely targets for take-over. When a frontal assault is blocked, climbers are likely to consolidate their present position or to move obliquely to increase their sphere of influence.

Conservers are antithetical to climbers. Where the latter are ever on the move, the former yearn to stand pat and maintain the status quo. Climbers welcome and foster change, provided it affords them opportunities to advance. Conservers resist and resent change, since it has an unsettling effect on well-structured and well-known relationships. Where the former seek power, the latter seek security and convenience. Climbers wish to break out and break through, conservers to dig in and hold fast to what they have.

Conservers tend to cluster at the middle management level, perhaps because they realize that they have gone as far as they are likely to go. They also tend to be found in organizations that rely extensively on formal regulations, protocol, and doing things by the book. It is interesting that the older the age of the key officials of an organization, the greater the number of conservers in it—probably, as Peter Drucker says, clinging to the crimson curse of red tape and bundling up yesterday in neat packages.

Zealots "have visions" and manifest an evangelistic zeal for the improvement of the organization—as they see it. Hence, they are single-minded, energetic, altrustic, aggressive, determined, and hard-driving. Unlike climbers, zealots have the interests and progress of the company at heart. Unlike conservers, they are impatient to improve and innovate. Their outspokenness is likely to irritate higher-echelon people who do not have the same visions. Opposition means little to zealots, who are more noted for their ability to bruise sensibilities than for their human relations skills. They are excellent instruments for stirring up an apathetic organization or getting a new one off the launching pad as speedily and vigorously as possible. They make far better task force leaders than overall administrators for the reason that they place their "sacred objectives" first and foremost, often to the neglect of other, more important goals.

Advocates are concerned for the improvement of the organization, especially the section of it they represent. They are tigers in fighting for their people and programs. Unlike zealots, who are basically loners, advocates are responsive to the ideas and influence of their superiors, peers, and subordinates. Unlike climbers, who are ever self-centered, advocates will at times promote programs that do not benefit them personally but have long-term favorable implications for the organization. Where zealots tend to take on all adversaries, advocates will engage in conflict only if supported by their colleagues. Externally, they defend their group or department in a partisan manner; internally, they are fair and impartial.

Statesmen, according to Downs, are generally found at the bottom and top of a given organization. They have an aversion to internecine warfare and petty politics, and they try to stand above parochial interests. They seek to reconcile factional clashes by pointing to the overall objectives or mission of the firm. They are found at the lower levels of the managerial hierarchy because few organizations promote statesmen; at the top, statesmanship is a requisite, since the incumbent must be above provincial affiliations.

A PSYCHOANALYTICAL VIEW OF MANAGERIAL LEADERSHIP

Erich Fromm has described diverse types of individuals, and Ernest Dale has adapted these classifications to different kinds of managers and executives.[3]

The receptive manager. The motto of the receptive leader is, "It is better to receive than to give." He does things not out of conviction but to win the approbation of others. He relies on others rather than himself to secure the good things of life. Weak and dependent, he finds it difficult to say no. This gets him into the hot water of conflicting loyalties and promises. For him, love implies being loved, not freely offering affection to others who deserve it. Left to his own resources, the receptive manager feels alone and helpless. Not surprisingly, he is usually submissive, friendly, adaptable, responsive, agreeable, and easy to live with. On the other hand, he is likely to be opinionless, unable to stand up and be counted, and perhaps overly eager to please and be accepted. Hence, he is normally a good worker and a fine producer, but innovation and the creative idea are beyond his talents.

The exploitative manager. The exploitative manager is a different breed of cat entirely. His motto is, "It is better to rape than to receive." He typically sets out to use, abuse, and manipulate others to satisfy his own ends. Everything and everyone are targets for raiding. Even when he is capable of coming up with good ideas or innovations, he seems to prefer to acquire them from others through cunning. People are to be squeezed for all they are worth, and their value is judged according to their potential for exploitation. If this sort of manager is self-confident, captivating, assertive, and capable of great initiative, he is also inclined to be arrogant, seducing, conceited, selfish, and grasping.

The hoarding manager. Like Downs's conserver, the hoarding executive follows the motto, "There is nothing new under the sun. Let's leave things the way they are." Well structured, pedantically orderly, supercautious, and methodical, the hoarder is concerned not so much with acquiring new and greater status as with sitting tight and holding fast to what he already possesses. Although he may be quite bright, little in the way of novel or productive thinking is likely to come from him. He frequently dominates his own people, and closeness or intimacy constitutes a threat. His ideal is a well-ordered operation with a place for everything and everyone in his place.

The marketing manager. The motto of the marketing manager is, "I will become as you desire me." Quite common in our culture, this executive experiences himself not as a unique human being but as a commodity. His end is not happiness but salability. If he is successful, then he feels worthwhile; if not, he feels worthless. He will say and do almost anything that promotes his success and progress. His interpersonal relationships are transient, superficial, and impersonal. His sense of identity stems not from an inner image but from the opinions that others have of him. In a sense, he is a chameleon, ready and eager to please the highest bidder. He can be sociable, competitive, undogmatic, open-minded, adaptable, outgoing, and purposeful. But he is also unprincipled, uninvolved, aimless, hyperactive for activity's sake, and endlessly concerned with the problem of suppressing an underlying sense of insecurity and inferiority. What is worse, since he has no firm moorings in goals or values, he may experience himself as a thing, become selfless, and thus be alienated not only from others but from himself as well.

The productive manager. The executive with a productive orientation is far from perfect. He suffers from the same slings and arrows of outrageous fortune as any of his colleagues. Yet he has a relatively clear notion of who he is and what he stands for. He realizes that the two central tasks of life are to learn how to give and receive affection and to gain satisfaction from meaningful work. He does not merely exist; he is committed to life and living. His motto is, "I may not be completely master of my fate or captain of my soul, but I certainly am not merely the victim of mindless circumstances." Accordingly, he has a sense of balance and proportion and resilience that enable him to experience ups and downs without overweening pride or despair. He has learned to come to grips with himself, with others, and with his environment. He seeks not only to actualize his potential but to contribute to the welfare of his fellowman and society at large.

Although there is no detailed scientific evidence to support the various classifications proposed by Downs and Dale, they have a ring of reality for the typical executive, who can readily supply names in his own firm for each of the categories. In fact, the average manager is likely to accept these descriptive types more readily than those produced by the tested research on leaders and leadership. Be this as it may, there are obviously no pure types, even though every executive's behavior is characterized by one or another major theme.

CHARISMATIC LEADERS

There is a frightening resemblance between the student "activists" of today, with their slogans of "idealism" and "sincerity," and the German youth movement just before and just after World War I. The resemblance even extends to externals, to long hair, to folk songs, and to such slogans as "Make love, not war." Yet the idealistic, antiauthoritarian *Wandervoegel* of the German youth movement—who also did not trust "anyone over thirty" —became in short order fanatical, dedicated, unquestioning Nazis and idolators of Hitler. The youth want and need faith. And the demagogue is the specialist in sincerity.[4]

Normally, one would give little thought to charismatic leaders. They go against the grain of a democratic philosophy of life. Yet they do arise from time to time. Accordingly, it is not so much the charismatic leader who should be the center of attention as it is the circumstances that produce him. What do we know about such leaders and the conditions that enable them to come to the fore? Robert Tucker[5] has summarized the genesis and characteristics of the charismatic leader along these lines:

1. The charismatic leader springs up during times of economic, social, political, or religious stress. He makes his move when long-established values are questioned or denied, when discontent with past traditions is painful, when customary ways of doing things fail, when a frustration-born desire for radical change is in the air, when disaster threatens.

2. A compelling magnetism and an overarching self-assurance are essential requirements for the charismatic leader. They enable him literally to cast a spell over his followers that prompts them to render him passionate alle-

giance, mindless enthusiasm, and blind obedience even when they may have doubts regarding certain ideas or actions he proposes.

3. He brings a message and a program that are evangelistic in their promise of salvation from the current impossible situation. His plan is simplistic and has great gut appeal. He is perceived by his followers as being almost mystically qualified to lead them out of their hopeless predicament, regardless of his objective qualifications to do so. It is this emotionalism that explains in large part an absurdity such as Hitler.

4. The magical message, which mesmerizes the unthinking (and which can often be supplied by skilled phrase makers), promises that things will become not just better but perfect. Charismatic leaders are experts at promising Utopia. Since perfection is the end, often the most heinous actions can be tolerated as seemingly necessary means to that end. In this sense, the extreme Right and the ultra Left form an unintended coalition in their attacks on the more moderate groups of any society.

5. It helps greatly if the charismatic leader can set up a straw man as the sole and solitary cause of all the troubles suffered by his followers. This not only has the advantages of oversimplification but also allows the rank and file to vent their venom on a clearly identified target for purposes of catharsis, while distracting them from the mistakes and frailties of the leader. Any handy scapegoat will serve this purpose, be it capitalists, the money changers of Wall Street, imperialists, the establishment, or what have you.

6. The charismatic leader may be morally good or evil. He may be a mere visionary or a hardheaded pragmatist. In fact, he may combine elements of both in his personality.

If charismatic leadership can be utilized for ethically worthy aims, what is so bad about it? First, it makes the followers far too dependent than is good for them in the long run on the so-called indispensable man; this is especially true in a democracy, where those who govern do so with the consent of the governed. Second, such leaders rarely if ever provide for their own succession; they assume tacitly that they will be here forever. Additionally, much of the energy and thought of the followers is likely to be channeled not into improving the organization but into currying favor with the leader. As a bishop was heard to comment after his consecration, "Now that I am a bishop, there are two experiences I shall never have again. These are to eat a poorly prepared meal and to hear the whole truth."

In an era when no one in his right mind would try to predict definitively what the next two or three basic social or cultural changes will be, it is prudent to hold in mind the dangers of seeking charismatic leaders. Today, traditional values and principles are being subjected to exacting scrutiny. Young people no longer bow down before the ideologies to which an older generation gave allegiance. Much is made of the "age of anxiety," the "aspirin age," the "identity vacuum," and "existential dread." *Alienation* is a commonly used term. Copouts from society abound. Accepted customs and mores are considered at best meaningless, at worst hypocritical or deadly. The defects of the private enterprise system are held up to scorn in some quarters and its contributions passed over in silence. While one is hardly likely to press the panic button simply because a minuscule minority is angry with a system that has benefited more people in more ways than any other in the history of the world, it behooves executives to be aware of the attraction of the charismatic leader, especially when he sings a self-aggrandizing siren song to seduce the unwary and the uninformed.

MANAGERIAL LEADERSHIP AS A PATTERN OF TRAITS

Tolstoy once remarked that all happy families are pretty much alike, "whereas each unhappy family is unhappy in its own way." As a projection of this observation, what would be more logical than to study the traits of outstanding leaders in the hope of gaining some insight into what differentiates prime movers from those who follow? Like many an idea that appears perfectly rational in the abstract, this has not worked out too well in practice.

The first problem has to do with the number of qualities that are proposed as essential for leadership. The lists vary from 5 or so to 20 or more. One at times gets the impression that the lists tell more about the enumerators than about the characteristics of leadership. To make matters worse, we know from factor analysis that many traits named are merely variations of a common dimension. One investigation indicated that no fewer than 17,000 one-word descriptions of leadership qualities were extant in the literature! Another reported that in 106 studies of leadership characteristics, only 5 percent of the traits appeared in four or more studies. And a close review of the literature concluded that numerous examinations of the personalities of leaders failed to produce any consistent pattern of traits. One can go on in this vein almost unendingly.

It is difficult to define traits that are mutually exclusive in operational terms. At times, contradictory qualities are included in the same listing, such as "forcefulness" and "tact." Even if the magical qualities were known, there would still remain the questions of what proportion of a set of traits is effective, how much of each is necessary, and in what situation a given trait is useful or harmful. The entire process is a fascinating exercise in frustration.

Even the most carefully done studies of leadership traits raise more questions than they answer. First, it is extremely difficult to define qualities in a manner that all will accept, much less measure them accurately. Second, it is impossible to avoid considerable overlapping among the traits. Third, the entire problem of the "product mix" of the qualities considered necessary or optimal for on-the-job success is left hanging. The practicing executive is perhaps better advised to deal with observed behavior than with abstract traits that seem simple but actually represent a semantic quagmire.

THE SITUATIONAL APPROACH

Some espouse a "great man" theory of leadership; others find the idea of an elite group convincing. Then there are those who lean toward a deterministic environment over which a man has little or no sway. Since the pendulum syndrome is common in human affairs, it is not surprising that as the efforts to unearth the qualities that guarantee leadership success prove less than productive, a reaction takes place and the situation is assumed to be responsible for a leader's rise. It is not so much a matter of a person imposing his personality on a situation as of the situation making it possible for the leader to emerge. Without World War II, for example, Dwight D. Eisenhower would have lived and died a respected but relatively unknown military professional. With World War II, however, he went on to become president not only of a noted university but of his nation. In another context, where would Franklin D. Roosevelt have ended up without the worst depression this country has ever experienced? At a more pedestrian level, a man might well become head of a firm not because he possessed the *relevant* competence but rather because he was fortunate enough to have the *relative* competence, being the son of the founder. Thus situationists stress not the characteristics of the leader but rather the group and environmental forces that enable a person to apply the qualities he happens to possess and thus exercise a needed leadership role. In a sense, it is much like making shadow figures by moving one's fingers between a light and a free-hanging sheet. Without the light and the sheet, the fingers would cast no shapes.

What Does It All Add Up To?

It seems clear from the discussion thus far that thinking of managerial leadership in terms of absolutes is largely futile. It is far wiser to think of it in terms of the interaction of several variables. The first is the personality of the leader. The personality structure of the typical executive is much too settled to alter radically. Whatever its configuration, it will make certain kinds of behavior easy for him to engage in, others hard, and still others impossible to carry off with finesse. This is evident from the analyses made by Downs and Dale.

As far as leadership characteristics are concerned, Bavelas summed up the matter neatly when he observed that there are *similar* qualities that tend to appear in a relatively broad spectrum of organizations, but there are also characteristics that are *unique* to each organization. Accordingly, an either-or approach is inadmissible. Certain so-called universal characteristics, such as intellectual acumen, prudently channeled initiative, resourcefulness, sensitivity to the feelings of others, and the ability to motivate and to communicate with impact, are always assets. But the way they are utilized must be guided by a careful assessment of the setting in which they are exercised. The manager–leader makes this assessment to ascertain the unique aspects of a given situation so that he may engage in appropriate behavior.

The qualities that the manager possesses or lacks are not nearly so important as his understanding of what kinds of behavior and which characteristics are likely to attract or alienate the work group. The entire notion of relying on the qualities that the leader should have represents an egregious misemphasis. Since it is the group he would influence, he must take his cues not from abstract research but from the persons and personalities who constitute the workforce. Finally, even the most outstanding personal qualities need a suitable arena to be exercised effectively. As the arena changes, together with the fields of force that it aggregates, the relative importance of this or that pattern of traits may be radically altered.

NOTES

1. Robert N. McMurry, "The Case for Benevolent Autocracy," *Harvard Business Review*, January–February 1958; see also Eugene E. Jennings, "Business Needs Mature Autocrats," *Nation's Business*, September 1958.
2. Anthony Downs, *Inside Bureaucracy* (Boston: Little Brown and Company, 1967), Chapter 9.
3. Erich Fromm, *Man for Himself* (New York: Henry Holt & Company, Inc., 1947); see also Ernest Dale, *Management: Theory and Practice*, 2d ed. (New York: McGraw-Hill Book Company, 1969), pp. 564–565.
4. Peter F. Drucker, *The Age of Discontinuity* (New York: Harper & Row, Publishers, 1968), p. 245.
5. Robert C. Tucker, "The Theory of Charismatic Leadership," *Daedalus,* Summer 1968, pp. 731–756.

LB
2805
G59

101278

Goode
Readings in educational management

Servire est vivare

LIBRARY